# THE DATING BLUEPRINT

## JASON EVERT

Totus Tuus
P R E S S

2019

**The Dating Blueprint**
**Jason Evert**
© 2019 Totus Tuus Press, LLC.

Unless otherwise noted, Scripture quotations are taken from the Revised Standard Version: Catholic Edition (RSV:CE) of the Bible, copyright © 1996 by the Division of Christian Education of the National Council of Churches of Christ in the United States of America. All rights reserved. If any copyrighted materials have been inadvertently used in this work without proper credit being given in one manner or another, please notify the publisher in writing so that future printings of this work may be corrected accordingly.

If any copyrighted materials have been inadvertently used in this work without proper credit being given in one manner or another, please notify the publisher in writing so that future printings of this work may be corrected accordingly.

Published by Totus Tuus Press, LLC.
P.O. Box 5065
Scottsdale, AZ 85261
www.totustuuspress.com

Cover by Devin Schadt
Interior by Russell Graphic Design

Printed in the United States of America

Hardcover ISBN: 978-1-944578-79-4
Paperback ISBN: 978-1-944578-76-3
E book ISBN: 978-1-944578-00-8

# CONTENTS

# INTRODUCTION

You've may already have noticed this, but we live in a culture of single people who pretend that they're dating, while the dating couples behave like they're married, and the married people seem to think they're single. Everything is out of order.

Much of the chaos is blamed on men, and it's fair to say that the culture is experiencing a deep crisis of masculinity. Men are often hesitant to commit. As a result, for the first time in history, the majority of Americans are unmarried. And corporations are losing a fortune because of the turnover rate of young adult men who can't make up their minds about their occupations.

It wasn't always like this. In 1942, my grandfather graduated high school and enlisted in the Army the next day. At the same age that I was playing ultimate frisbee in college, he was flying into thunderstorms at night in World War II to dodge fighter aircraft. On one of his missions, while delivering a cargo load of barbed wire past hostile forces below, one of his engines failed. As the plane's altitude was dropping, he and the crew began frantically throwing the entire load out the back door to lighten the warplane's weight, lacerating their arms and hands in the process. Landing wasn't an option because they were in Japanese territory three hundred miles behind enemy lines in Burma, and the camp below took no prisoners and would have slaughtered them. In the midst of the chaos, he offered a prayer and immediately the engine restarted.

Like the other 16 million soldiers who served in World War II, he returned home knowing what mattered in life. Asking a woman on a date wasn't a risk; being shot out of the sky was. He returned with a sense of purpose, proposed to his high school sweetheart, raised ten children, and enjoyed a sixty-six-year marriage. Today, he rests in peace, sharing a tombstone with the woman he insisted was the most beautiful bride ever. And if that's not enough, their names were Joseph and Mary. Not bad.

Perhaps because men aren't forced to grow up as quickly as they were in the 1940s, we've lost a sense of urgency and direction. Even the icons of masculinity offered to modern men are lacking in depth. Bishop Thomas Olmstead points out:

> "For decades now, a model for manhood has been fashioned in the fictional British spy character named James Bond. Various actors have taken turns portraying this man who, in several adventures, has proposed what it means to be 'manly,' yet Bond remains an enigma. Like the women that he uses in the films, the ones who watch him find themselves wanting to know him. He is never a father, nor does he accept responsibility for or love one woman. In him, we see a man whose relationships are shallow and purely utilitarian. Indeed, 'James Bond is a male character whose name is the height of irony. He is 40 years old and has no bonds. He is actually pathetic.'"[1]

Men learn manhood from men. This is the way cultures have always operated. But with the breakdown in the modern family and the virtual extinction of dating, young men rarely see authentic examples. When it comes to courting a woman, many men are proficient with dating apps but aren't sure how to look a woman in the eyes and hold a meaningful conversation. What's needed is a clear and simple step-by-step guide.

I once read a meme created by women that stated, "When you guys give us directions, don't use confusing words like

'East.'" While such particulars might not be helpful to some women, men appreciate precise instructions.

Unfortunately, when it comes to dating, the only time men receive specific guidelines is when they're being told what they're *not* supposed to do. As a result, very few know what they *are* supposed to do! They're given generalities like "Be a gentleman." But this is useless. We want a map, a compass, a manual!

One reason such a blueprint doesn't already exist is because women don't feel comfortable telling a man what they wish he knew about dating. They just expect him to know it. Therefore, I decided I would stand in the breach. I figured: "I already found my wife. Maybe women will tell me what they want guys to know, and I can pass it on to the men!"

It worked.

Looking at the analytics of our social media accounts, I saw that more than one hundred thousand young women follow our content. So, I posted a few videos for them, explaining that I wanted to write this book for men. I wanted to know, from a woman's perspective, the answer to questions such as: How would you want to be asked out on a date? How would you *not* want to be asked out on a date? What habits or vices would you want a man to overcome before he dates you? If he's not interested in continuing the relationship, how do you want him to communicate that to you?

I asked the women to post their comments, promising that I'd read every one of them and integrate their thoughts into the book.

Boy, did the floodgates open! Within minutes, hundreds of women from around the world had left their feedback. Within a few days I'd received well over a thousand responses. In total, they generously submitted more than thirty thousand words of feedback. It took awhile, but I scoured through every word because I owed it to them, as well as to you.

After reading all the comments, the first thing I thought was: I wish someone had told me this a long time ago! Dating would have been so much simpler if I had just known what I was supposed to do (and what I wasn't supposed to do). Therefore, it brings me great joy to share this book with you. My hope is that it will help you to find your bride and become the man she deserves for you to be.

# 1

# LOVE YOUR BRIDE
# BEFORE YOU MEET HER

Imagine a college student who saw the woman of his dreams during his freshmen orientation social. When he noticed her across the room, their eyes met briefly and his heart skipped a beat. He *knew* that he *had* to meet her. Nonchalantly, he maneuvered his way toward her and struck up a conversation. Her personality was as radiant as her smile, and it felt as if they had already known each other for years. He attempted to contain his excitement when he learned from her that they would be sharing a class together. That night, he could hardly fall asleep, knowing that he had all semester to look forward to seeing her on a regular basis.

A few weeks later, he knew she would be coming through his dorm with some of her friends on a Saturday afternoon before they all went to the game together. Thankfully, he had plenty of time to prepare for her arrival, and for this critical first impression of his personal life.

As she passed through the threshold of his doorway, the stench of fermenting laundry wafted through the air. Crumpled empty bags of ramen noodles were strewn on the floor near the overflowing trash can, and his desk looked like someone had overturned his entire bookshelf onto it. Atop a small refrigerator sat a pizza box containing a few leftover pieces of hardened crust and a cup of empty garlic sauce from a late-night delivery a few nights earlier.

The young women stepped into the room, making sure that they didn't trip over the tangled mass of wires from his video game console that stretched across the floor. Pausing, she took in the scene with her friends, trying to breathe through their mouths to avoid gagging on the smell of his gym clothes, which were piled so high that one would think he was waiting until Thanksgiving break to have his mom sanitize them.

Thankfully, this isn't a true story (I cleaned my dorm room before any women saw it). However, it's a painfully accurate analogy of how countless men approach their dating relationships. Although their exterior life might be in order, their interior life often resembles the dorm room described above. In other words, they enjoy the idea of bringing a beautiful woman into their lives, but they've done nothing to prepare themselves for her arrival. Therefore, if you feel called to marriage, it is essential that you learn how to love your bride before you meet her. Here's how.

## Catch the Foxes

If you've ever read the Bible from beginning to end, about halfway through you'll discover the Song of Songs, which is erotic love poetry. Although the book doesn't mention God, it is a profound analogy of the depth of His love. It is structured as a duet between the lover and his beloved bride. Although many of the phrases sound awkward to today's ears—such as when the man tells the woman that her hair reminds him of a flock of goats—there are some jewels of wisdom within its pages. One such example is when the man tells the woman, "Catch us the foxes, the little foxes, that spoil the vineyards, for our vineyards are in blossom."[2]

In this passage, the vineyard represents their love, which is flourishing as the two prepare for marriage. However, in order for it to thrive, the couple must be vigilant to eliminate all that threatens it, namely the foxes that eat the grapes, gnaw at the branches, and dig up the roots. What a modern man can glean from this passage is that he and the woman have been entrusted with the task of guarding love against all that would contaminate and undermine it.

A man's first step in doing this is to make a sober assessment of his interior life. In other words, are there habits or vices that he has developed as a single man that would be toxic to his future vocation? A man ought to consider this before he begins a relationship, or immediately if he's already in one.

In order to make progress in expunging one's faults, general resolutions are worse than ineffective—they're harmful. The reason for this is that if a man commits to "being a better person," he feels as if some kind of progress is being made. But without a clear diagnosis, an ailment cannot be treated, and the prognosis is likely to worsen. Without a clear goal, tracking progress is impossible. Therefore, begin by naming the issues. Is it alcohol or drugs? Is it pornography and masturbation? What about excessive gaming or self-absorption? Whatever the case may be, call it out and go after it.

Although a man's shortcomings may be evident to him, sometimes to helps to get input from others. So, I asked approximately five hundred women the following question: What is the number one fault that you would want a man to root out of his life before he enters a dating relationship? Some of the replies were interesting, such as: "Not meeting his ex-girlfriend at the duck pond." (Not sure what that was about.) Other replies were more enlightening.

Out of the hundreds of suggestions, a significant number of women said that the biggest issues were selfishness, laziness, pride, excessive gaming, or infidelity. However, there was one issue above all that women hoped a man would conquer prior to dating them, and they mentioned it nearly four times as often as any other topic: pornography (and masturbation). Because it was such a predominant theme in their replies, it's important for men to have an effective strategy to win the battle. As tempting as it may be to pass over this subject and skip ahead to the more exciting details regarding women's thoughts on dating, it must be treated in depth in order for a man to love a woman rightly.

## No Excuses

Once a man identifies a vice within him, the temptation often arises for him to dismiss the need to uproot it. At times, this temptation manifests itself as sloth, or acedia, which is the sadness that arises from the realization that what is good is also difficult. When sloth begins to take root within a man, he will excuse himself from making any serious effort to change. He may say to himself, "There's no rush. I'll overcome this eventually."

Or, he may justify his behavior because others are doing worse things. Because every man has heard other guys joke about pornography and masturbation incessantly ever since they were at the seventh-grade lunch table, males are tempted to assume that this is an inevitable part of being a man. When we consider what others are doing, we compare ourselves favorably to them.

We may begin to consider one type of pornography more permissible than another. For example, a young man asked me about a friend of his who had a habit of looking at animated porn. He assumed that because there were no actual women involved, no one was being harmed. In his mind, he could obtain his enjoyment without degrading anyone in the process. But here's the problem: Humans are made for love, and anime characters will never provide this. Men are created to make a gift of themselves, but if a man wastes his life lusting after cartoons, he'll miss the point of his existence.

It may seem like a laughable anecdote, but when a man justifies his behavior, there's a problem. We all do this in different ways, even though we know that virtue never requires rationalization. We know that if we make excuses for our faults, we'll never overcome them. Instead, they gradually obtain the upper hand. One man noted that when we extinguish the capacity for guilt, "man then becomes inwardly hardened and sick."[3]

Sometimes, we retreat into self-pity, which is a common symptom that comes with the illness of lust. Indulging in lust with our minds, eyes, and bodies makes us men who pity ourselves when our cravings aren't being met. It turns us into spoiled children. We'd like to think we're manly men who just have needs, when in reality we've grown quite soft.

One rabbi noted, "At first, sin is like an occasional visitor, then like a guest who stays for a while, and finally like the master of the house."[4] He added that sin is not merely a temporary lapse in the strength of the will, but actually weakens the will until it is crippled. All along, we tell ourselves that we're free not to make these choices, but our freedom slowly dwindles as we become servants to our vices.

## Slay the Beast

A          n once confided in me that when he         
f          end, he watches twelve hours of por

on Saturday, then goes to bed. He wakes up on Sunday and watches about twelve hours more. Looking down at the floor, he added, "I don't even enjoy it anymore. It disgusts me, but I don't know how to live without it."

Upon hearing his story, some men may be tempted to look upon themselves with a sense of satisfaction that they're not *that* addicted. But it may surprise you to learn that the frequency of a behavior doesn't determine one's level of addiction. Rather, addiction is measured by our inability to resist the behavior, regardless of how frequently the desires arise.

But the problem with lust is not that it can be addictive. C.S. Lewis summed up the issue well when he wrote about masturbation. He said:

> "For me the real evil of masturbation [would] be that it takes an appetite which, in lawful use, leads the individual out of himself to complete (and correct) his own personality in that of another (and finally in children and even grandchildren) and turns it back: sends the man back into the prison of himself, there to keep a harem of imaginary brides. And this harem, once admitted, works against his *ever* getting out and really uniting with a real woman. For the harem is always accessible, always subservient, calls for no sacrifices or adjustments, and can be endowed with erotic and psychological attractions which no real woman can rival. Among those shadowy brides he is always adored, always the perfect lover: no demand is made on his unselfishness, no mortification ever imposed on his vanity. . . . After all, almost the *main* work of life is to *come out* of our selves, out of the little, dark prison we are all born in. Masturbation is to be avoided

as *all* things are to be avoided [which] retard this process. The danger is that of coming to *love* the prison."[5]

There are several reasons that explain the allure of lust, but Lewis makes some keen observations about it. Masturbation teaches men to think, "Why do I need another? I can satisfy myself, without having to concern myself with someone else's needs. I don't have to worry about another person's willingness or acceptance." With pornography and masturbation, the fantasies require nothing from the user. He's safe because he can't disappoint the image. It can't look back at him with anything other than eyes filled with seductive awe. Therefore, rejection and embarrassment are taken out of play—as long as no one catches him in the act. The pixels won't say no. They're always available, ready to cater to his desires. There's a façade of connection, affirmation, desirability, and acceptance that briefly satiates his deep yearnings for these things. But then, like the mirage of a desert oasis, the fantasy vanishes. What had seemed like a blazing inferno moments earlier turns into a pile of ashes, leaving him cold and still waiting to give and receive authentic love. He feels restless and disturbed. Instead of finding satisfaction, he may experience an inner disgust toward himself and a gradual resentment toward women.

If this is the sad state of a soul after falling for the counterfeit of love, then why does it seem so easy to fall back into the same habits? There are a number of reasons. For one, underneath lust is a desire for love, a longing for beauty, intimacy, companionship, and pleasure. All these things are from God, and it is natural for a man to desire them. The problem is that pornography takes these good desires and pollutes them with lust. Imagine a man who was dying of thirst and came upon an algae-infested swamp. He would feel a desire for what was good (the water), while having a repugnance for all that distorted its goodness and purity. Yet, if there was no better offering, he might drink. The same thing is happening in terms of pornography and masturbation. Therefore, the problem with pornography is not just that a man is using a woman, but that the man himself is being used! Someone else is profiting by selling him a counterfeit of what he really desires.

Another reason why men fall into the habit of viewing pornography is that few boys are ever taught how to respond to the degradation of women. I once read a book on fatherhood in which the author recommended that dads should instruct their boys how to react vigorously against pornography if someone shows it to them. He suggested:

> "It is best if a boy hears from his father that he should take charge of the situation by rejecting this great evil in some way, whether smashing a phone, ripping a picture, or even screaming something like 'This is sick! Get away from me!' In these ways a boy can actively reject impurity rather than be paralyzed by it. . . . We need to help our sons understand that there is a time for a violent and strong reaction against anything that presents women in the wrong way."[6]

Aside from thinking about how many cell phones would be destroyed on a daily basis if boys took this to heart, what's your reaction when you read this father's advice? We may be more concerned about the condition of the cell phone or the reputation of the screaming boy than we are about the woman being exploited. This is a trained response.

Think about it: How many boys receive such counsel from their fathers? I'd wager less than 1 percent! In fact, the father-son relationship is one of the most common ways that boys encounter pornography. Many of my friends began their addictions by sneaking looks at their father's porn collection. Another was told by his winking dad, when he discovered the boy's personal magazine stash, "Don't worry about it. Just don't let your mom know." I know another who was brought to a brothel by his father, and congratulated afterward with the words, "Now you're a man."

Really? Once upon a time, a man was someone who conquered himself for the sake of a woman, and now we become men by conquering women for our sakes?

It's time for men to regain their ability to vigorously reject the degradation not only of women, but of the gift of human sexuality itself. Christianity demands such a response. You will notice that when Our Lord speaks of the battle against sin, he uses violent imagery, saying that a man should be willing to cut off his hand or pluck out his eye rather than sin.[7] Obviously, Jesus is not condoning mutilation as a remedy for sin. Rather, he's expressing a deep truth: Sin is serious. It is more damaging to the human person than losing an eye or hand. The injuries sustained by the soul are more costly than those to the body. Yet, we pamper our bodies and become careless with our souls.

To kindle a sense of urgency in your battle against sin (no matter what the vice may be), consider what you truly desire. If you hope to become a husband and father one day, think of this as your kingdom that stands off at a distance. Within its gates, your bride and your future children await your arrival. However, standing between you and the entrance is a beast that cannot be ignored or tamed. If you attempt to maneuver around it and enter your castle, the wretched creature will follow you into the fortified city and wreak havoc on all its inhabitants. Until the thing is defeated, it is too dangerous for you to enter. Therefore, you have two viable choices: either remain indefinitely at a distance, hoping it dies of old age before you do, or slay it and walk past its corpse.

## Get to the Root

Although some men fall into lust because they were never taught to vigorously reject it, a more substantial cause might be that they're trying to address the *fruit* of the problem rather than its *root*. For example, consider the man who has struggled for years unsuccessfully to break free from pornography. Although he's tried a number of internet filters and apps, he always manages to find a way around them when the temptations are strongest. He's trying to pluck the rotten fruit (lust) without addressing its root.

If you want to discover the root of any vice, consider your state of mind when you fall. Are you bored, lonely, angry, stressed, or tired? When these deeper needs are not being met, we often attempt to satiate them with false consolations. Psychologist Jeffrey Satinover explains:

> "The filling of a false need leads to a temporary experience of pleasure which, for a time, overrides the genuine need it is hiding. *But the genuine need is not being met.* After an invariably short time, then, the original distress returns, stronger than ever for having remained wholly unaddressed. The transient experience of pleasure provides but the illusion of fulfillment; the disillusionment only sharpens the true need. Immediately the craving returns, again and again, and soon

a habit has been established: the habit of turning to the fulfill-ment of the false need whenever the true, underlying distress is aroused. And it's always aroused because it's never filled."[8]

For example, when a man experiences loneliness, what does he do? Does he retreat into his phone for hours of mind-numb-ing stimuli? Or, does he seek out healthy friendships? If a per-son's true needs are fulfilled, the appeal and fascination of lust will lose much of its power.

Temptation is strongest during moments of desolation. But what a man chooses to do at such times is a great indication of his affective, or emotional, maturity. The age at which he begins turning to pornography, masturbation, alcohol, sex, wasted time online, etc . . . to deal with life's problems will be the emotional age at which he will remain until a new pattern of life is established.

This is one reason why pornography is so detrimental to a man's character development. For the first nine months of his existence within his mother's womb, a boy experiences the woman's body as a source of consolation. When he enters the world, the first consolation he knows is the woman's body, as he is drawn to the breast of his mother. As a toddler, again he will seek his mother's embrace during times of uncertainty or suf-fering. Through a process of maturation, a boy is weaned from this maternal comfort, and by the intervention of his father, he learns to face the trials of life independently. Soon, he will become a source of strength and consolation to women.

Pornography interrupts this entire process of masculine development, sending the man back to the body of a woman as a sensual refuge when he encounters the difficulties of life. Instead of being a source of consolation to women, he begins to see her body as something that will bring him consolation. If a man uses fantasies as a way to cope with stress, then he'll use the stress as an excuse to indulge. Such emotional immaturity often erupts within marriage, due to the fact that marriage entails significant levels of stress.

This atrophy of masculine development usually doesn't manifest itself in the earliest stages of a romantic relationship, because that season of love tends to be characterized by excitement and hopefulness. However, when the demands of love begin to assert themselves and the initial infatuation begins to taper off, the man often finds himself unprepared and disoriented. I know of some husbands who were successful in removing their pornography habit prior to marriage, but never took the time to heal from its effects. When challenges arose within marriage, they began questioning their vocation altogether, savoring the memories of the life they once led.

When such a crisis arises, the solution isn't to flee one's post, but to retrace one's steps and heal the roots that were never addressed. The process is a long one and will require patience and perhaps counseling. But in time the man will discover that one does not simply make good decisions by being strong. One becomes strong by making good decisions.

## Spiritual Defense

If you're going to succeed at any sport, a game plan is essential. When I played Little League baseball as a child, I didn't have one. I recall standing in the outfield, daydreaming about dinosaurs and chewing on my leather mitt. Whenever someone hit the ball in my direction, I'd pick it up and throw it toward whichever infielder seemed most excited.

By the time I played college baseball, things had changed. Before every pitch, I considered the tendencies of the batter during his last plate appearance, the number of outs, the position of base runners, and where I would throw the ball depending on whether it was hit in the air or on the ground. Because I knew what to do before each pitch was thrown, I was prepared for the outcome.

When it comes to the spiritual life, many Christians lack defensive strategies against the daily temptations that assail them. When lustful thoughts arise or tempting images appear, they always feel as if they are caught off guard. They may have been told to "bounce their eyes" when they see an attractive woman, and there is indeed merit in keeping custody of our eyes if we can't look at a woman without lusting. But is there more to purity of heart than avoiding the sight of beauty?

Beauty is an invitation to love, and therefore it demands a "yes" rather than simply a "no." But how does a man respond affirmatively toward a woman who presents herself in a manner that seems to invite lust rather than love? Here's a four-step plan that can be implemented at any moment. You can use it when lustful flashbacks occur in your imagination, when you see a seductive advertisement, or when you're tempted to stare at a woman in a way you shouldn't.

## Step one:

Begin by making a small and inconspicuous sign of the cross on your forehead with your finger. To anyone watching, this will appear as if you're scratching an itch or resting your head in your hand briefly. But this is an external sign of the interior prayer you're about to offer. The fourth-century Christian writer Saint Basil of Caesarea noted that the sign of the cross was a tradition taught by the apostles themselves, and the earliest Christians testify to its widespread use.[9] It was not merely a sign, but a statement and a seal against evil.

You will notice that the first motion of the sign of the cross is upward. Use this to remind you of the first response you should have toward beauty: *gratitude*. When you see a beautiful woman, thank God for her. He is the architect of her body. The devil did not invent the feminine form. He can only distort our ability to view it as God intended (as an invitation to love). So, rather than feeling a neurotic tension between your sexual desire and God's plan for your holiness, stop. Say thank you. You could even pray Psalm 84:1, which reads, "How lovely is thy dwelling place, O Lord of hosts!" But don't stop with a prayer of thanksgiving.

### Step two:

The second motion of the sign of the cross is downward. This is a reminder of your need to offer a prayer of contrition. For example, "God, I am sorry for the times I have not looked rightly upon your daughters. Create in me a clean heart."

### Step three:

The third part of the sign of the cross moves to your side. This is your reminder to bring your thoughts back to the woman. Her beauty demands a response of love, and now is your opportunity. Look at her left hand. Does she have a wedding ring? If so, pray for her marriage. If she does not, pray for her future vocation. Transform temptation into intercession. Even if the temptation is a memory or fantasy that begins to emerge, you can still pause and pray for all women you may have viewed in the past with lust. You never know where they are in their lives at this moment, or how much they may need your prayers.

One might even think of this as a form of spiritual Tai Chi. This is a martial art that absorbs or redirects the opponent's aggression and uses that force against him. Therefore, instead of allowing temptation to lead you closer to hell, you seize the opportunity to lead the subject of your attraction—and yourself—toward heaven.

This step is not only beneficial to the woman who receives the grace from your prayer, it also helps to heal one of the wounds that pornography inflicts upon a man's imagination: the depersonalization of the woman. Although porn stars are the center of all the attention in pornography, they're almost invisible. In other words, their bodies eclipse their humanity. What would happen to the global pornography business if it revealed more than the woman's body? What if it showed the woman herself?

Take, for example, Pamela Anderson. She was a global icon within the pornography industry and had mastered the ability to hide her wounds under a cloak of sensuality. At age forty-six, she exposed more than pornography ever could during a speech at the Cannes Film Festival:

"I did not have an easy childhood. Despite loving parents, I was molested from age six to ten by my female babysitter. I went to a friend's boyfriend's house and when she was busy the boyfriend's older brother decided he would teach me backgammon, which led into a back massage, which led into rape. My first heterosexual experience. He was twenty-five years old, I was twelve. My first boyfriend in grade nine decided it would be funny to gang rape me with six of his friends. Needless to say I had a hard time trusting humans and I just wanted off this earth."[10]

She's not alone, because every woman in the industry has her own story. I know of another who realized she needed to quit after her fourth abortion. For these reasons and countless others, these women need for heroic men to respond to their beauty with loving intercession rather than lustful craving.

Jesus said that at the final judgment each man's fate will be determined by actions such as: "I was naked and you clothed me." When a man clothes a woman with dignity and prayer, he is clothing Jesus Christ, who sometimes comes to us in a disguise of broken humanity. As he said, "Truly, I say to you, as you did it to one of the least of these my brethren, you did it to me" (Matt. 25:40).

In the end, the only antidote to lust is love. Therefore, the only solution to pornography addiction is love for porn stars. A shame-based approach to overcoming our urges will never stand the test of time. Yes, we should avoid the sight of anything that reduces a woman to her sexual value. But something very truthful is missing if the message never goes beyond this. The body is "very good."[11] God said so.

Since the dawn of creation, the beauty of the human body has been an invitation to love. When Adam and Eve first gazed upon each other's nakedness, they saw their call to love one another through making a total gift of themselves. However, nowadays this divine calling to love descends to mere lust. If you feel that you lack authentic love for women, ask God for a share of the love he has for his daughters. Keep in mind that the goal of purity isn't to annihilate our desires, but to set them ablaze with divine love. Purity of heart isn't about becoming numb to beauty, but about having the ability to see the woman fully.

## Step four:

The final movement in the sign of the cross is to move across
the body toward the other side. Think of this as moving your
thoughts from the woman's beauty to the source of the beauty
she reflects, which is God. Have you ever noticed that when
men stare at a beautiful woman, their facial expressions look as
if they've never seen one before? With each experience of feminine beauty, we unconsciously feel an echo of Adam's original
awe at the creative work of God.

Each discovery of beauty feels unique because it is a finite
reflection of the infinite beauty of the Blessed Trinity. Despite
the allure of femininity, there is always a restless craving that
follows, because her beauty—no matter how intoxicating—is
only a glimmer of the ultimate beauty that the human soul has
been created to experience in heaven.

Therefore, the beauty of the woman is not an end in itself.
One theologian explained:

> "Indeed, an essential function of genuine beauty, as empha-
> sized by Plato, is that it gives man a healthy 'shock,' it draws
> him out of himself, wrenches him away from resignation and
> from being content with the humdrum—it even makes him
> suffer, piercing him like a dart, but in so doing it 'reawakens'
> him, opening afresh the eyes of his heart and mind, giving
> him wings, carrying him aloft. . . . Beauty pulls us up short,
> but in so doing it reminds us of our final destiny, it sets us
> back on our path, fills us with new hope, gives us the cour-
> age to live to the full the unique gift of life."[12]

Not only did God bless women with beauty, a man's desire

for beauty is also a gift from God! What many men never realize is that sexual desire is not the same thing as lust. They imagine that when they reach a pinnacle of perfect chastity, their sexual desires will be extinguished. But the absence of desire is not an indication that a man is holy; it means he's either unconscious or deceased. Our human desires are meant to point us toward God, not away from him. Perhaps this is why the devil invests so much energy distorting our perspective of the body.

While pornography—and all sin, for that matter—leads to isolation, love draws us toward union. By praying for our temptations instead of simply against them, we're uniting ourselves in love to the women in this life. And with perseverance, we can be united with them for all eternity in heaven. But viewing women rightly also brings us into a deeper union with God, reminding us of the One who truly deserves our worship and adoration. Persevere in doing this, and you will encounter God where you least thought you'd find him.

## Victory Awaits

The ultimate goal of purity is not simply the absence of pornography, but the presence of a pure heart. A man isn't called by God to simply keep his desires in check, but to relearn how to relate to women, so he can be free to love. Women long to find this capacity in a man. They yearn to experience what has been called "the peace of the interior gaze."[13] This is the security and tranquility of heart that a woman feels when a man looks at her with authentic love. Its opposite is the restless vulnerability that many women know all too well, which causes them to guard their hearts and bodies. After all, if a man is not the guardian of a woman's dignity, she'll need to assume the role he has abandoned.

Good men yearn to possess such integrity of heart, but many wonder if such a goal is attainable. Many have fought valiantly against their sexual addictions for years and feel like they've hardly made any progress. They feel as if they're swimming upstream and getting nowhere. What they don't realize is that if they stopped swimming, they would float downstream like a dead fish. There's life in the struggle.

Should you feel this way, know that God is with you in the fight. He is not in the clouds, waiting to judge you. Jesus Christ is within your soul, striving in you toward purity. It's not you versus the devil, with God as the spectator. It's you and the Blessed Trinity (with all the hosts of heaven) against hell. Those are good odds.

Without question, you are engaged in battle with evil itself. Although modern minds often dismiss the reality of the devil, claiming that he is only a literary symbol of evil, keep in mind that Jesus didn't have conversations with symbols.[14] He didn't cast out symbols, and he wasn't tempted by a symbol the desert.[15] Nonetheless, the devil appreciates when men dismiss his existence, because he can work all the more effectively against them. Ignatius of Loyola's Spiritual Exercises provides a classic tool in understanding his tactics. In this sixteenth-century masterpiece, he presents three strategies used against us by the enemy of our souls, which are worth quoting at length. (The first might sound a bit sexist to modern ears, but give him a pass and soak in the deeper message.):

1. The enemy conducts himself as a woman. He is a weakling before a show of strength, and a tyrant if he has his will. It is characteristic of a woman in a quarrel with a man to lose courage and take to flight if the man shows that he is determined and fearless. However, if the man loses courage and begins to

flee, the anger, vindictiveness, and rage of the woman surge up and know no bounds. In the same way, the enemy becomes weak, loses courage, and turns to flight with his seductions as soon as one leading a spiritual life faces his temptations boldly, and does exactly the opposite of what he suggests. However, if one begins to be afraid and to lose courage in temptations, no wild animal on earth can be more fierce than the enemy of our human nature. He will carry out his perverse intentions with consummate malice.

2. Our enemy may also be compared in his manner of acting to a false lover. He seeks to remain hidden and does not want to be discovered. If such a lover speaks with evil intention to the daughter of a good father, or to the wife of a good husband, and seeks to seduce them, he wants his words and solicitations kept secret. He is greatly displeased if his evil suggestions and depraved intentions are revealed by the daughter to her father, or by the wife to her husband. Then he readily sees he will not succeed in what he has begun. In the same way, when the enemy of our human nature tempts a just soul with his wiles and seductions, he earnestly desires that they be received secretly and kept secret. But if one manifests them to a confessor, or to some other spiritual person who understands his deceits and malicious designs, the evil one is very much vexed. For he knows that he cannot succeed in his evil undertaking, once his evident deceits have been revealed.

3. The conduct of our enemy may also be compared to the tactics of a leader intent upon seizing and plundering a position

he desires. A commander and leader of an army will encamp, explore the fortifications and defenses of the stronghold, and attack at the weakest point. In the same way, the enemy of our human nature investigates from every side all our virtues, theological, cardinal and moral. Where he finds the defenses of eternal salvation weakest and most deficient, there he attacks and tries to take us by storm.[16]

Take some time in prayer to digest the wisdom offered above. Ask yourself: How seriously have I resisted my inclinations that tempt me to be less of a man than God has created me to be? Have I hidden my faults from the light, in order that they might not be exposed? Have the defenses of my soul been breached? When we are timid in our response to temptation, too prideful to expose our wounds, and lax in keeping our souls fortified, the enemy won't simply harass our spiritual fortress externally, but will seek to invade and infest it. Our untreated wounds and vices become not simply a gateway to evil, but an invitation for it. Perhaps it's time for doors to be shut and a formal disinvitation to be issued.

When the devil sees you getting so close to the finish line, he will attempt to make you think you're farther away than ever before, to keep you from taking those next few strides. Persevere. At times, you may feel hemmed in by God's moral laws, but realize that the Grand Canyon was not formed by a stagnant swamp without boundaries, but by a raging river hemmed in by solid rock. You're the raging river, with all your passions and desires. You need the rock that surrounds you (God's law), so you don't turn into a lifeless and stagnant swamp. If the rock and the river stay in place, they create something beautiful.

As tempting as it may be to focus on the struggles of the present moment, raise your eyes. Think about what kind of legacy you want to leave your children. Imagine if you were to surrender to the struggle and resign yourself to the fact that lust will always have dominion over you. Indeed, you'll have your share of pleasure over the next several years and decades of your life. But is this your deepest desire?

If you have ever seen the movie *Braveheart*, you will recall the moment when William Wallace exhorts those who were wavering in their desire to sacrifice their lives in battle:

> "Yes. Fight and you may die. Run and you will live, at least awhile. And dying in your bed many years from now, would you be willing to trade all the days from this day to that, for one chance to come back here as young men, and tell our enemies that they may take our lives, but they will never take our freedom?"

It's no different with the struggle for self-mastery that every man experiences. Stay in the fight, and you'll face suffering. But there is no dishonor in being wounded in battle. The only dishonor is when a soldier leaves the battlefield. After all, what's the alternative to a life without pornography and masturbation? Defeat and mediocrity. You were created for more.

## Everything is at Stake

While climbing down a slot canyon in southeastern Utah, outdoorsman Aron Ralston dislodged an eight-hundred-pound boulder that tumbled for a moment before crushing his right hand against the interior wall of the canyon. For the next five days, he employed every conceivable method to free his pinned limb, but to no avail. Exhausted and dehydrated—and forty pounds lighter than when the accident occurred—he began to waver in and out of consciousness, resigning himself to the fact that the footsteps of death were near. He carved his own epitaph into the wall of the cavern, filmed a goodbye video to his family, and began to hallucinate.

During his vision, he saw a boy who was no more than three years old walking toward him. Although Aron wasn't a father yet, he knew that this child would eventually be his son, whose very existence depended upon his escape. When the premonition vanished, Aron fashioned a tourniquet and proceeded to amputate his arm with a dull pocket-knife. Using the torque of the boulder against his own weight, he snapped his radius and ulna. After wrapping his arm to control the bleeding, he hobbled out of the cavern into the light, where a Highway Patrol helicopter rescued him. As fate would have it, he eventually met his met his bride-to-be, Jessica, and they welcomed their first child into the world . . . a boy. Several years later, the account of his harrowing experience became the movie *127 Hours*.

While Aron was trapped in the cavern, he spent several days considering whether he should amputate his arm. However, he wasn't motivated to act upon the idea until he realized that the life of his child depended upon his willingness to suffer. The liberation that Aron brought upon himself was only made possible through a radical sacrifice that was ignited by love. Love alone had the power to set him free.

Likewise, when it comes to the topic of sexual addiction and pornography, countless vocations hang in the balance. Although not all men are called to marry, how many marriages today do not exist because potential suitors have been too entranced by laptop fantasies to bother with the demands of commitment and the fears of rejection? Imagine how many children have not been born because their would-be fathers never matured into men. And imagine how many generations of descendants do not exist today—and will not exist for all eternity—because the men who would have brought them into being were too enamored by the distractions of this world to assume the demands of a family. All of this is at stake. The destiny of countless souls depends upon a man's willingness to love.

Therefore, if you feel called to marriage, take a moment to imagine your future bride and family. They already possess an extraordinary power to draw you out of the shell of egocentrism that you may feel inclined to retreat into. For love of them, do whatever you need to do in order to liberate yourself from lustful habits and any other vices that prevent you from being the man they deserve.

When it comes to finding and building a relationship of authentic love, marriage preparation does not begin with the engagement. Such a mind-set could be compared to a man who desires to become a professional athlete by practicing diligently six months before the draft. He's already a decade late. Therefore, begin now. If you want love, *focus on becoming the man that God is calling you to be, not on finding the woman you want him to give you*. Don't obsess about finding the perfect bride. Grow in perfection to become the man she deserves for you to be.

## 2

# IS SHE THE ONE?

To pass the time while riding the bus to elementary school, my classmates and I would sometimes pass around sheets of paper to play the game MASH. The acronym stood for Mansion, Apartment, Shack, and House, and offered an amusing means to predict the future of one's love life. Just as there were four potential future housing options, one could list four potential future spouses, four cars, and up to four children.

Through the game of chance, any number of potential outcomes could be revealed. You could end up living in a shack with your sixth-grade crush, driving a Lamborghini, and raising four children. Needless to say, it wasn't the most accurate way to forecast our future vocations, but it offered no small amount of entertainment during the otherwise monotonous bus ride.

As trifling as the game may have been, it made us all wonder: Where do I want to be in a decade? Who do I want to end up with, and what do I want my life to look like? These questions have existed in the heart of every young person in history. But of all the possibilities that existed within MASH, the one question that elicited the most excitement wasn't the sports car or the mansion, it was the person: Who is the one for me?

This is a timeless question, and if we don't know where to look, discovering the answer can be a heartbreaking and frustrating process. However, it doesn't need to be overcomplicated if you follow a clear blueprint:

*Discern if she's the right woman to date (and if it's the right time to date). Then, pursue her with sincerity and commit to her with clarity. That's it.*

Later chapters in this book will explain how to pursue her with sincerity and commit to her with clarity. But before that can happen, the man must do some discernment work. To do this, consider the following grid:

Obviously, the goal is to find the right woman at the right time. What's a man to do if this doesn't happen? Consider the other three scenarios:

If you meet a woman who seems like the right one, but it's not the right time to date, focus on the friendship and give it time.

If it's the right time to date, but a woman doesn't seem like the right fit, again, focus on the friendship.

If you meet a woman and it's not the right match or the right time, don't move beyond friendship.

However, all of these questions beg the big question: How can you know when the two align? Here's how:

## Is She the Right Woman?

Over the course of your life, you'll be attracted to countless women. Some of them would make wonderful spouses, while others would be disastrous to date or marry. How do you know the difference, especially when the allurement of physical beauty can so easily blur your judgment? Below is a list of ten essential questions to ask yourself in order to make a wise choice. Although it's not possible to know the answers to all of these questions if you're just getting to know someone, make sure to find the answers to them before you commit to a serious relationship.

### Do you know what you're looking for?

Men and women often find themselves in unhealthy relationships that take off like a rocket, and then proceed to descend like one. One of the root causes of this predictable pattern of failure is that people don't take the time to consider what they're looking for in a relationship. If a person is merely looking for a good time, any number of partners will suffice. If they're looking for someone who is available and attractive, a significant slice of the population fits the description. But this isn't asking enough.

The purpose of dating is not recreation or to solve the problem of loneliness. The purpose of dating is to find a spouse. In short, it's like a job interview where you need to know the qualifications you're looking for in the other. Therefore, create a mental list. When my wife was single, she asked herself why she had ended up in so many dead-end relationships. Her answer was that she didn't have a list. So, she made one: a list of sixty-one qualities she wanted in a future spouse. Some were nonnegotiable, while others were wishful thinking.

After making the list, she didn't have a date for three years. She had plenty of offers, but she wasn't interested in mentoring boys into men, turning them into personal projects. This list became like a wall around the castle of her heart. Because of it, she was free when I met her. She wasn't simply available—she was living her life to the full, without compromising for less than she truly desired. Therefore, make your own list of qualities you hope to find in a future spouse. But more importantly, become the list.

### Does she possess virtue?

I've heard it said that the man who marries a virtuous woman will have a happy life, even if she is not the most attractive woman he has ever seen. However, the man who marries the most attractive woman on earth will have a miserable life if she lacks virtue. For this reason, Scripture admonishes men to remember: "Charm is deceptive and beauty fleeting; the woman who fears the LORD is to be praised."[17] This is not to say that physical attraction is not important. It is. But it's not the most important.

## Can you see her as more than a girlfriend?

By this question, I do not mean whether you can see her as a wife and mother. Obviously if a man cannot imagine a woman in this way, then he has no business dating her. What I mean is: Can you see her as a friend and sister rather than only a potential future girlfriend. This is easier said than done when physical attraction is involved. It involves a conscious effort to keep your mind and heart in check, so that you can enjoy a woman for who she is, rather than for who she might become for you.

By not getting too far ahead of yourself, you will be better able to build a graced foundation of friendship—and that's what holds marriages together better than anything. Take your time during this stage, because when couples become "more than friends" without spending much time being friends, they typically become less than friends.

## Does she share your faith?

Although some people marry others who do not share their faith, this arrangement will always create challenges unless neither partner cares about their religion. So long as at least one of them cares about spirituality, a mixed marriage will present difficulties. For example, in which faith will the children be raised? Is she willing to celebrate your wedding in your church rather than hers? Will she be willing for you to teach the children religious truths that she does not believe? Will the children prefer her religious service to yours? Are you able to pray together as a family without tension? These are questions that need to be answered now rather than later. If you feel passionate about wanting to share your faith with your spouse, this consideration needs to be taken into account before you date, instead of expecting her to convert.

Missionary friendships are a great way to evangelize, but missionary relationships create an awkward dynamic. As the couple progresses in their relationship, odds are that at least one person is hoping the other will change his or her mind. When this expectation doesn't materialize, they may find themselves years into a relationship and feeling like they've reached an impasse.

When you weigh the importance of this matter, remember that the decision about who you date will not only impact you. It's a decision for your children as well. Therefore, give them a godly mother. She doesn't need to be a saint yet. If she has a sincere desire to be one, that's enough.

## Are you in agreement on moral issues?

Men and women often ask me, "How do I talk to my girlfriend/boyfriend about my beliefs regarding sex before marriage?" Upon hearing this, I wonder: "How did you end up dating someone without knowing what they believe about such an important issue?"

These discussions should not surface within a dating relationship. They should be sorted out long before commitment takes place. This is one of the functions of the friendship phase of courting a woman. It's a time to build intellectual intimacy by sharing thoughts, beliefs, and values. Before committing to a woman, you want to make certain that the two of you are in agreement on serious moral issues. It's not time to celebrate the diversity of your ethical viewpoints. You want to know if you can build a life together on sound moral principles. Does she agree with you about the purpose and meaning of human sexuality, family planning, pornography, abortion, etc.? Obviously, these aren't first-date conversation starters. But if the two of you do not see eye to eye on what kind of life is true, good, and beautiful, then it will be difficult to build such a life together.

### Do you share a common view about your goals for a family?

Plain and simple: If you envision driving a cargo-size van filled to the brim with a multitude of homeschooled children, and she prefers to wait until she's in her early forties to begin a family, you need to think twice about dating. Again, this isn't a topic you bring up on date number one. It's something you gradually learn about each other.

Overlooking the answer to this question can cause a lifetime of tension and regret. I know of one man who always longed for a large family, but his girlfriend didn't. He assumed that her heart would soften with time, but the opposite took place. She only became more sure of her choice, and although they married, they had only one child. It has been a great cause of sorrow for him, but since childbearing required a bit of cooperation on the woman's part, her decision prevailed.

### Does your relationship have a good history?

The best indication of the future of a relationship is its past. During the courtship phase of a relationship, couples are typically on their best behavior. Therefore, take a good look. If your friendship or dating relationship with a woman involves a pattern of instability, distrust, drama, disrespect, infidelity, or fighting, it's likely that these problems will persist. Don't expect that marriage will resolve any of this. If anything, marriage will trigger more of the same issues because stress levels are greater within family life.

If you notice negative behavior patterns in the relationship now, keep track of them. Perhaps make a written log. While you can argue with your memory and airbrush the past, it's much harder to refute history when it's in your own handwriting. Perhaps the issue is getting better. Maybe the two of you have hit a tough spot in the relationship and you simply need to work through it. Sometimes counseling can give you both the push needed to break through this barrier together.

On the other hand, be honest with yourself if matters aren't improving. Perhaps there's an underlying issue that isn't being addressed. Maybe there are deeper psychological concerns that will require thorough counseling to resolve. If both people are invested in healing the issue and moving forward, there is hope. If there's no serious resolution or plan to break an unhealthy pattern in the relationship, don't move forward. Without true healing and wholeness, it isn't time for dating.

In the meantime, if she is facing significant personal or psychological struggles, it's fine to maintain a friendship with her through the process. However, don't try to be her messiah and rescue her from deep personal issues. Put down your cape. She needs to pursue healing for her sake, not for you. Besides, it has been said that if you try to rescue a damsel in distress, you'll merely end up with a distressed damsel.

### Do the people who love you also love her?

During the initial stages of a relationship, men and women always form an idealized image of the other. Part of this is because infatuation and attraction blur our judgment. But it's also due to the fact that every person enters relationships with a host of expectations about who we hope the other person might be. When you add to this the fact that many people scour their prospective partner's social media accounts, they often think they know the person better than they do. The challenge is that our expectations of a person often get in the way of seeing them for who they truly are. Then, if you add physical intimacy into the mix, one's objectivity is gone.

Such immediate closeness obscures our judgment. It could be compared to reading a book that's only an inch away from your eyes. Only those who hold it at a distance are able to read it with clarity. In the same way, sometimes those who are further removed from our relationships can see them better than we can. Therefore, don't discern your future with a woman alone. Tap into the wisdom of your family, close friends, spiritual director, counselor, pastor, accountability partner, and everyone else whose opinions you trust and respect.

When we fail to do this, and instead discern alone based on our personal perceptions, we often begin to play God and attempt to predict the future. We may assume that the intensity of our emotions is an indication of our destiny. We might be tempted to justify the expression of spousal love before being espoused. Then, if the relationship does not end as we had expected, we may find ourselves bewildered and inconsolable. To avoid all of this, stay grounded and make sure that the people who love you also love her. But make sure they love who she truly is, not simply who they think she is. Spend ample time together in the company of family and friends, so that those who love you can form a balanced viewpoint on the strengths and weaknesses of your love.

## Are you attracted to more than her physical beauty?

Imagine if every woman on earth looked exactly like the woman to whom you are attracted. Can you honestly say you would feel drawn to her? What is it about her that draws you to her? Do you truly admire her? Does she bring out the best in you? Does she inspire you to grow closer to God? Does she make you want to become a better man, and even a saint? Do you like who you are when you're around her? Take the time to mull over this one, to ensure that you're attracted to more than her physical beauty.

## Do her parents have a strong marriage?

This question feels almost unfair to consider, because there's nothing a woman can do to impact how her parents relate to one another. But the question is worth asking because this is the main relationship that she has witnessed for the better part of two decades. Does her mother treat her father with respect and affection? Is her father faithful and tender toward her mother? Can they disagree while still being reverent toward each other? Do they enjoy being in each other's company? Do they speak well of the other? If so, the woman you're interested in has been blessed with a tremendous advantage in her own relationships.

If the answer to many of these questions is no, and her parent's relationship is fractured or riddled with conflict, it doesn't mean that you need to break things off with her. What it means is that you need to proceed with patience and caution. If the woman you're interested in never witnessed a functional marriage in her own home, has she had the opportunity to learn from a good couple elsewhere? If she never saw a woman who could fully entrust her heart to a man without being wounded or guarded, does she feel prepared to do this herself?

Although these are difficult questions to ask, they're not deal breakers. Just because a woman's family of origin isn't ideal does not mean that she's incapable of building a beautiful family of her own. However, it will require significantly greater effort on her part.

## Is it the Right Time?

If you feel that you've found the right woman to pursue, it does not necessarily follow that it's the ideal time to date. This needs to be discerned as well. Just as I offered ten questions above to give clarity on *who* to date, it is equally important to know *when* to date. Here's how:

### Are you prepared to be available?

When I was a child, I begged my parents for a dog. Although my mother abhorred such creatures, my years of pleading prevailed and they eventually gave me one. In my eyes, my one responsibility toward the animal was to play with it whenever I desired. Needless to say, as the fecal matter began to accumulate in the backyard and the lawn furniture was being gradually gnawed into pieces, my parents were underwhelmed by my caretaking abilities, and the pooch was history.

Unfortunately, many people enter dating relationships with the same level of maturity. They see a girlfriend as something they really want to "have," without taking into consideration the proper care and feeding of another human being. Therefore, before focusing on your desire to be in a relationship, discern whether you are ready to give a woman the time and attention she deserves. If you don't have the time and energy that are required to invest in lasting love, do not initiate the request.

## Are your motives sincere?

Before you ask a woman into a committed romantic relationship—or even on a date—one of the most essential words to keep in mind is *intentionality*. As a father might ask a young man who wishes to date his daughter, "What are your intentions with my daughter?"

Therefore, be transparent. Ask yourself: Why am I doing this? Why do I want to pursue her? Do I see her as a potential future spouse? Are there superficial motives in play, such as the satisfaction of lust, the thrill of the chase, the elevation of my social status, the alleviation of loneliness, or the satisfaction of my curiosity? Or, can I say that I have integrity in my desires? Do I sincerely want to get to know her better in order to discern marriage together? Do I intend to pursue her in an honorable way that would not bring any hurt to her, her family, or her future husband (if I'm not him)? If you cannot say with certainty that your motives are in the right place, then it's not time to date.

## Are you ready emotionally?

Are there any emotional issues that you're currently wrestling with that could be an impediment to forming a healthy bond with a girlfriend or future wife? For example, if you have struggled with depression, sexual abuse, or family brokenness, have you sought counseling to heal from these experiences?

If you feel negative emotions welling up within you, don't ignore them. Allow yourself to feel them, rather than trying to control them in order to appear stoic or happy. When you attempt to stuff your negative emotions instead of dealing with them, it has the same effect as covering up the gauges on your car's dashboard so that you'll never have to see that the engine is overheating, the fuel is low, or the oil needs to be changed. The lights (negative emotions) go on because something needs attention. Take care of any serious warning lights before dating.

## Are you prepared spiritually?

When you enter into a committed dating relationship, the goal is to discern the will of God together. But if a man does not know how to listen to God's voice before a relationship, entering a relationship won't automatically change this. Likewise, if a man does not know how to guard his own purity without a girlfriend, he won't be prepared to guard hers. When they're together, she'll end up being the one who has to draw the line because he'll be unprepared to direct the relationship toward God.

If the man struggles with pornography, he might even assume that such unfaithful behavior should be tolerated by women. It's not enough for him to drop his porn habit when the girlfriend demands it. He needs time to heal from its effects. Therefore, a man should be free from addiction before dating, and should have gone at least several months without a relapse. He must solidify his decision to choose a person instead of pixels, because he can't have both.

Although renouncing sin is an essential first step, time is still needed to heal from its effects. Imagine a man who jumped into a fire, and then regretted his choice. His level of regret doesn't accelerate the healing of his body. In the same way, sin leaves its mark, and healing takes time.

## Have you had a sufficient break since your last relationship?

If you have recently ended another relationship, have you taken enough time to recover? Some people date the way a frog hops from one lily pad to another, avoiding the space in between. But such individuals are not freely giving themselves to others. Rather, they are using other people as pacifiers to alleviate any feelings of loneliness.

If you've been in a recent serious or long-term relationship, don't rush into another. Take time to heal. How long? Every situation is different, but perhaps a good rule would be to take a break for at least half the length of the past relationship. So, if you dated someone for a year, take at least six months off before starting something new. This isn't a fixed rule, especially after very long relationships. The point is to take adequate time to emotionally reset.

### Is this a long-distance relationship?

While there are countless advantages to the internet, one of the great disadvantages is that many couples are starting relationships with the odds stacked against them. Some individuals fall in love four thousand miles away from each other, without a realistic plan for how they will manage to live in the same hemisphere at any point within the next decade.

On a more local scale, countless high school students initiate serious dating relationships, seemingly unaware that graduation looms on the horizon. When summer arrives, many young men have shared with me how they felt caught off guard, wondering what they should do for the next four years, while their girlfriend moves to the other side of the country to meet thirty thousand new friends . . . and then lands a job in another state. They wonder, "Do we just break up? Do we try to make it last?"

There's no easy answer to these dilemmas, and there are certainly high school relationships that have bloomed into lasting marriages. There are couples who met from across the globe online and are equally happy. What's not often seen, though, are all the situations where it didn't work out. The lesson to be learned here is not that long-distance relationships are impossible. They're simply less probable and desirable. Therefore, before you pursue a woman, it's best if she lives in the same area code. The main reason for this is because although two people might *meet* online, *dating* needs to take place face-to-face.

Likewise, in terms of high school relationships, there's a great deal of wisdom in delaying the onset of dating. With college around the corner, remember that long-term, long-distance relationships are difficult to maintain, whereas long-term, long-distance friendships are not.

### Is marriage reasonably within reach?

If the purpose of dating is to find a spouse, then the proper time to date is when marriage isn't too far off. For example, if a couple begins dating when their potential future wedding is still a decade away, they're probably hurting their chances of ending up together. Instead of rushing into romance, such a couple would do well to focus on enjoying the simplicity of their friendship without progressing so quickly into a committed dating relationship. By doing so, they're not passively waiting for their love to ripen. Rather, they're building a sturdy foundation for it. They're giving themselves a better chance for the relationship to bloom when the time is right.

### Do you both know how to be alone?

Two upright lines can be brought much closer to each other than two diagonal ones. In the same way, couples who know how to live happily independent of one another will be capable of a closer unity than couples who can't stand on their own two feet without the other.

Although singleness can be a difficult state for men as well as women, it is essential that we find a reasonable amount of purpose and meaning to our lives without waiting for a significant other to fill that void. In an article published in *The New York Times*, one man observed: "We think constant connection will make us feel less lonely. The opposite is true. If we are unable to be alone, we are far more likely to be lonely. If we don't teach our children to be alone, they will know only how to be lonely."[18]

This skill is remarkably useful within dating relationships. When individuals who don't know how to be happy alone enter a relationship, at first their constant devotion to the other may feel flattering. But it may soon suffocate the other. If a flame is to be kept alive, it needs oxygen. It needs room to breathe. In the same manner, relationships need space to thrive, and if your girlfriend is your everything, it will be too much for her to bear.

## Is she ready?

While a man can discern alone that he's ready to date, he must remember that there's another person's life that must be taken into consideration. All of the above points apply to the woman as well. Is she available, emotionally and spiritually ready, and so on? Each person must discern on their own, and then take a leap of faith to begin the process of discerning together.

As I once read in an old dating booklet from the 1940s, "Yours is an unbelievable lot, brother. You are required to decide for the rest of your life, at a time when you are bereft of reason." Therefore, to make a wise choice regarding a future spouse, absorb as much counsel as possible and then be decisive.

## Don't Grasp

Perhaps one of the greatest temptations during the single stage of one's life is to grasp. We're tempted to make things happen on our own timeline. When the right woman and the right time never seem to align, we may wonder what we're doing wrong. We may feel as if God has somehow abandoned us along the way.

Therefore, what's needed more than anything is trust. It can be frustrating when the future isn't unfolding according to our plans. But waiting on God is a means through which He sanctifies us. We may have no idea where he is leading us, but this doesn't mean that he's far from us. Our holiness is not measured by how well we predict the future, but by how patiently and peacefully we wait for it to unfold. Therefore, don't be quick to grasp for what you think you want. Have the courage to let God bring it to you in his time.

Don't give God a deadline. Some attempt to do this through prayer. They think, "I want to know what God's will is, so I'll say a prayer for nine days and wait for my sign." The problem with this approach is that God often doesn't work this way, and if we expect him to do so, we end up looking for signs outside of us instead of listening to his voice within. Therefore, instead of praying that you would *understand* God's will, it is more important to pray that you would *do* his will. Do this, and he'll take care of the rest.

In the meantime, put God first. When I met my wife, she and I were both deliberately not dating. Instead, we were taking time off in our lives to focus on what God wanted us to do. We both felt that he wanted us to promote chastity, and that's how we met—at a chastity conference in the Bahamas!

In the Gospel of Matthew, Jesus says, "But seek first his kingdom and his righteousness, and all these things shall be yours as well."[19] However, we can't say, "Okay, God. If I need to put you first in my life in order to get what I want, then I hereby declare you first. Now can I have what I want?" It doesn't work like that.

If you are being called to marriage, then your future spouse deserves for you to be the best person you can be. Therefore, your single years aren't meant to be spent in anxious waiting. Keep your eyes on him rather than on potential future spouses, and you'll discover his will for you much more efficiently. Trust him, because God doesn't simply want more from you, he wants more for you.

# ASK HER OUT!

## Save the Date

"It's easy to hook up with someone you've just met in a dark room after having a few drinks. But asking someone out on a date in broad daylight, and when you actually have to know their name, can be really scary."[20] This was the candid response of a Boston College freshman when his professor, Kerry Cronin, invited her students—as a class assignment—to go on a date. Another raised his hand and inquired, "How would you ask someone on a date? . . . Like the actual words?"

Despite the fact that the vast majority of college students report that they would rather have a traditional romantic relationship than a hookup, they are twice as likely to hookup as they are to go on a first date.[21] When researchers gave a questionnaire to 187 college students asking how they feel about themselves after a hookup, 5 percent said they felt proud and a grand total of 2 percent felt desirable or wanted.[22] If that's the case, then why do so many settle?

Numerous explanations play a factor, such as the allure of pleasure without the demands of commitment, the risk of heartbreak, the time constraints of a serious relationship, societal pressure, and so on.

However, one major reason why men don't ask more women out is that they simply don't know how. Or if they do, they're afraid she'll say no. They hide behind their cell phones, using the screen like a shield that can buffet any potential blows of unacceptance. So, they download apps that can do the work for them. Swiping this way and that, they avoid the cumbersome work of looking a woman in the eyes, conversing with her, and discerning her level of interest and availability.

Considering how many women a man can browse through on his phone, it may strike some as not merely old-fashioned but outright inefficient to look for one in public. Besides, it's infinitely easier to accept rejection over a phone than in person. As an added perk, some men get away with saying and sending things through the phone that would get them slapped or arrested if attempted in public.

Ask any woman, and they're sick of it. But they go along because the commercialization of dating has become the predominant social script. I would propose that instead of following the script, men and women alike have a duty to rewrite it. Instead of pointing fingers and assigning blame, what is needed is a fresh blueprint for how to approach relationships. We already discussed above the importance of discernment when it comes to pursuing a woman. Once a man has done his work there, what's needed is action.

Action is the most overlooked stage of discernment. At some point, speculation needs to end, and an investment must be made. A risk needs to be taken. The die must be cast. Without this, a man will forever remain in a state of paralysis by analysis. Because of a lack of certainty, he holds back and refuses to commit and move forward. But one of the traits of authentic masculinity is decisiveness. This does not mean that a man is stubborn and nonnegotiable. It means that he has the courage to make up his mind, act, and accept the consequences of his choice.

## Risk it All

At the age of sixteen, I pulled my truck out of a church parking lot and began the drive home. Sitting beside me was the high school girl I had quietly admired for months. She was beautiful, popular, holy, fun, a homecoming queen nominee, and for all intents and purposes, entirely out of my league. However, she happened to live near me, and we (I) agreed it made sense to drive together to youth group.

Homecoming was approaching, and so I decided I would give it a shot. I knew that if I didn't desire a woman enough to face the fear of rejection, I simply did not desire her enough. With my heart pounding, a nervous lump in my throat, and sweaty palms clinging to my steering wheel, I asked her if she'd go with me to the dance. For whatever reason, she immediately said yes. Over the next few years, we went to several more dances and became closer friends . . . and then she married a friend of mine. Regardless, I look back upon that night with a sense of contentment and pride. Had I never asked her out because I was afraid she'd say no, I would have allowed my fears to dictate my fate. But a man is called to do the opposite.

In recent decades, the idea that it's the man's job to initiate a relationship has been renounced and retired. Women should be free to make the first move, they say. It shouldn't matter, the argument goes, who asks who out, or who proposes to whom. But here's my take: It does matter, and it is the man's job. While such a statement might produce an anaphylactic reaction in some people, there's a reason why civilization has functioned this way for millennia.

Historically, men have been tasked with initiating love because it takes the fear and burden of rejection off the woman and places it squarely upon the shoulders of the man, where it belongs. It's not a sign of male dominance, but rather an act of respect for women. It's similar to the timeless expectation that when a gentleman walks on the sidewalk with a woman, he should place himself between the woman and the street. Should a car be driving too close, or a vehicle splash water toward them, it's preferable for him to take the hit. What kind of man would want to stand anywhere else?

Some may argue that the idea that a man ought to initiate love is simply a gender stereotype, stemming from patriarchal norms and cultural conditioning. But what if it's the other way around? What if God stamped into every man's body not only his identity, but his mission? What if cultural norms emerge from who we *are* as male and female?

To validate this theory, consider the body of a man. What distinguishes him from "the fairer sex"? For one, he possesses a unique strength. On average, men have 36 percent more muscle mass than women.[23] Ninety percent of women have a grip strength that is weaker than 95 percent of men.[24] Obviously none of this means that men are superior. But if God has created our bodies to be meaningful, this tells us he desires us to do something good with this strength. Furthermore, a man's body is created to initiate the gift of life-giving love. Unfortunately, many men misuse their masculinity to dominate and manipulate women, initiating sterile lust instead.

However, when a man becomes who he is, he will initiate love, commit to his beloved, create life with her, and sustain what he has created. These marks of masculinity are not simply how a man *should* act. They are who the man *is*. Consider the societal results when a man never lives out this calling, or begins the process and quits: What happens when a man initiates love but refuses to commit? The result is a culture of lonely women and emasculated bachelors. What if the man commits, and is too fearful to create life? His society is doomed. What happens when a man creates life, but doesn't sustain what he has created? The result is abortion and single moms who live under the poverty level with their fatherless children. In short, everything is at stake.

Such talk might strike some men as a bit extreme and even apocalyptic. Others might realize the logic of it but feel intimidated by the level of responsibility required of them. While it's true that not every man is called to marriage, all are called to make a gift of themselves in a way that gives life to others. However, for any number of reasons, men hold back. More often than not, there's one underlying cause that needs to be called out: a false notion of freedom.

## False Freedom

Without pausing to consider the fact that humanity would cease to exist if people took her seriously, MSN author Linda Melone published an article titled "10 Reasons You Should Never Have Kids." In it, she offers a number of data points that justify limiting one's family size to zero. For example, she explains that if you have children, "a large part of your life will be focused on your relationship with your child, rather than yourself." Heaven forbid.

She added that if you don't have kids, you'll receive health benefits because "You won't be exposed to germs your kids bring back from daycare. . . . Primarily, you get aches, pains, flu like symptoms and diarrhea." On this point, her argument is sound. My children bring home Ebola in their lunchboxes. But it boosts your immune system.

She goes on: "You'll spare yourself from back pain from lifting and carrying babies . . . lifting a baby out of a car seat and into a supermarket cart tax your core muscles and can lead to back pain and other injuries over time." Finally, she rejoices that without children, "You can be alone any time you want . . . If you don't have time to yourself you end up losing yourself." She quotes an expert: "Not having kids means you won't lose yourself. You can play tennis, do yoga or whatever you want all the time."[25]

This article might seem laughable, but the mentality is ubiquitous. After the birth of our third child, I returned to my gym, and one of the men on the basketball court greeted me, "Hey, we haven't seen you in a while!" I explained to him that we just had a little girl. He knew I already had two boys, and looked at me with shock: "Three!? You've got your girl now, so you're done, right?" I wanted to reply, "Yes, I have collected all the genders. I can stop procreating now."

Had I told him we were buying a third car, I'm sure he would have been happier for us. What ever happened to "Congratulations"?

What happened is that men have been sold a false notion of freedom. It begins during the single years, when a young man is told that he might be better off if he refuses to commit to one woman. After all, what if someone better comes along? "Enjoy your independence. Who wants to be tied down? Settle down later. Much later." Once he eventually chooses a woman, marriage means "game over," and the wife is considered to be a "ball and chain." Instead of deciding into marriage, they often slide into it after months or years of hesitation and cohabitation.

This view of life overlooks the fact that freedom is not an end in itself. It is a good, but it exists to be given away for the sake of love. Consider the life of a soldier: For the love of his country and family, he leaves behind the freedoms of civilian life to serve in the armed forces. He surrenders his liberty so that others might have theirs. Such a man isn't living in fear. He's free to live for others because he isn't a slave of self-absorption. True freedom requires such fearlessness. In the words of G.K. Chesterton, "Most modern freedom is at root fear. It is not so much that we are too bold to endure rules; it is rather that we are too timid to endure responsibilities."[26]

The ability to make a gift of himself is the unmistakable mark of a man who is truly free. In the same way, when a man surrenders the "freedom" of the single life in favor of committed love, he discovers something every man knows at his core: We desire love more than we yearn for freedom. When freedom from commitment becomes our goal, we miss out on the love we were created to give and receive. As Karol Wojtyła said, "Take away from love the fullness of self-surrender, the completeness of personal commitment, and what remains will be a total denial and negation of it."[27]

If a man rejects this false notion of freedom and has done his work discerning who to date and when to date, all that remains is for him to act.

## Dating: What a Woman Wants

As I mentioned in the introduction, as part of the research for this book, I surveyed more than a thousand women to gather their thoughts on the essentials a man needs to know about dating. For starters, I wanted to know, from a woman's perspective, the answer to two questions: How would you want to be asked out on a date, and how would you NOT want to be asked out on a date? Here's what they said:

### Ask her in person.

When I asked the women how they did *not* want to be asked out, perhaps the top reply was, "Do it in person and NEVER, NEVER, OVER TEXT." Others said, "Asking through a text is super lame." This sentiment was universal. What's the problem with texting? I'll let them explain:

"A text doesn't take much. Really putting yourself out there, and showing her that you're serious with your intentions, and not playing around sets the tone and an understanding for the both of you going forward: you're not playing around here. This is real!"

"Texts are artificial. A real girl wants a real relationship."

"He has to ask in person, it's the same logic that he has to get married in person and not over phone or video conferencing."

"I feel like guys these days rely on social media and texting to avoid having to make real social interactions and relationships."

"Work up the courage. It's too easy to hide behind a screen these days."

Although getting rejected via text might be less painful for a man than being rejected in person, women explained that texting *increases* his chances of being rejected!

"So many guys out there take the easy way out going on all these dating apps just to send a message. But the issue there is that this avenue is quantity over quality . . . Just an FYI to guys: It's much harder to turn you down if you're standing in front of her asking instead of behind a screen."

"LET ME JUST SAYYYY. The easier it is to ask a lady out, the easier it is for the lady to say no."

The same goes for social media:

"Honestly if a guy asked me for my social media instead of my number, that makes me uninterested right away."

"No matter how he asks me out on a date, if he ends with, 'Let me get your [social media],' it's an instant no for me . . . Gotta get my number."

While asking through a screen decreases your chances of her saying yes, asking her in person has the opposite effect:

"I think giving her a call instead of texting shows confidence in a man . . . which is attractive!"

"I do NOT want to be asked out over a text, it's cowardly and not sincere. The guy is trying to take the easy way out if he gets rejected. If anything, I'll probably decline the offer, even if I do want to go out with the guy, only because he asked over a text. Now vice versa, if a guy were to ask me out in person, and me not want to go out with him, I would probably give it a shot just because he was confident and up for the challenge."

"It's also adorable and warms my heart see the victory motion some guys do. The men seem to feel more accomplished when they hear the yes, asked in person, than when hiding behind a screen and reading the word yes."

### Use the word "date."

If you care about a woman's heart, understand this: Clarity is charity. As adamant as women were about not wanting to be asked out through a screen, they were equally universal in their disdain for being asked to "hang out," "chill," "meet up," "get together," or some other ambiguous phrase. They desire a man who is clear, intentional, and simple in his request. As one woman put it, being vague "doesn't exactly make a girl go weak at the knees."

Others added:

"Lots of guys will ask us if we want to 'hang out.' No, we don't want to hang out. We have plenty of girlfriends to hang out with. What we want is for you to take us to do something fun that allows you to get to know our personalities and allows us to get to know yours!"

"Do not say, 'Do you want to hang out?' I have had several guys ask me that and it's so frustrating because it leaves me wondering 'Are we just two friends getting together or is this a date? Is he trying to pursue me? What is this?' It's so confusing! I would much rather a guy say, 'Hey I'd really like to get to know you better. Could I take you out on a date?'"

"Girls already overthink enough as it is. He can't be afraid to be bold and be vulnerable, clearly and genuinely asking her out!"

"I know 'going for coffee' sounds like you just asked her out, but her mind is spinning, wondering if he meant it to be a date or just a friendly hangout."

"The worst is going on a 'date' and going home and wondering if it was a date to him or not."

"The best thing a man can be when asking a woman out is CLEAR! Super-duper crystal clean clear."

"As long as he is CLEAR on what he wants, he wins."

One thing I discovered when reading through the comments was how desirable it was for a woman to hear the word "date." This was one of the most prevalent themes in all of the suggestions that the women offered. One reason why women appreciate this is that the word is clear. There's no need for her to guess what he is trying to say.

"Use the word 'date'! Even if you are just interested in getting to know her first, not necessarily ready to ask her to be your girlfriend. Literally any other way of phrasing it leaves a girl slightly confused."

"We women like to be pursued. When you ask us on a date, please actually call it a date. I know much better what to expect, how to act, and how to dress for the occasion. If you are going to flatter me by risking rejection to ask me on a date, I ought to at least return the favor by dressing for the occasion."

"The man should be clear about his intentions. There should be no doubt in the woman's mind that she is being asked on an official date."

"Don't use words or phrases like 'hang out' or else in my mind, if I am romantically interested in you, that leaves me confused and anxious. That anxiety can be too overwhelming and then I cope with that by not expecting it to be a 'date' because that wasn't the word you used anyways."

"Even the simplicity of 'Would you like to go on a date with me?' is amazing. No vague coffee outing first. Take me out for date, not to your house."

Another reason why women appreciated the use of the word "date" is that it made them feel valued because the man was taking a clear risk by asking her out:

"It shows me he's willing to take a risk for me AND take

initiative. That's the kind of man I would want to raise my future kids with!"

"This communicates to me that I am worth the risk to be potentially rejected."

"Asking a lady on a date can't help but put a man in a position of vulnerability. There is risk. I think this plays into how God made us by nature and that is a good thing!"

"Please be the one to initiate and pursue. Leaving her to do that is unnatural and will create unwanted confusion and drama."

"Rejection is a part of life. Anyone who has ever tried to land a job knows it. But avoiding rejection by using loose or 'chill' phrasing to blunt the blow to the ego is not the answer."

Finally, women expressed their desire for a man to be intentional in asking her out:

"And above all, NEVER flirt just for flirting's sake. It's disrespectful to flirt with a girl just because it's 'fun' and not have any intention to pursue her."

"Don't date if you're not ready to commit to a relationship. Do not date if you don't know the true purpose of a relationship either."

"Don't flirt for a while and just expect the relationship to form out of thin air when nothing official was asked or discussed."

"I don't like it when guys LOOK for a girl to date. Patience is key. You cannot be desperate because dating is a discernment to marriage. You can't go into it thinking you want to date just for fun."

## Be friends first.

Although one woman said, "I think in this day and age it is so courageous for a man to walk up to a woman, strike up a conversation, and ask her on a date," the vast majority of the women stated that they don't prefer this approach. For example:

"I usually say no when a guy I met only once or twice asks to hang out one-on-one because you aren't sure of their intentions."

"Don't ask out a girl you barely know or just met. There's less of a chance we'll say yes to going on a date with a guy we barely know."

"You gotta become a friend to me before you ask me out. I have to know you and feel comfortable around you. Never just come up to me having never talked to me before and ask me out because that will never work."

"I did not want to be asked out. My husband befriended me first, and it escalated from there. He then asked my dad, and officially asked me. That's how I wanted it to be done . . . and I married him."

"I would never want a guy to ask me out so soon after meeting him . . . I would want a guy to be friends with me for a while before he asks me out on a date, and ask in a respectful way."

"Warm up with friendship first, depending on where you meet, trying to get acquainted on a friendship basis is always good so that the girl can be more receptive. If a guy immediately asks me out, I get a little creeped out."

The women gave a generous amount of feedback regarding the importance of friendship before romance:

"Be friends enough to know what sets her apart from other women and makes you interested in her rather than someone else. You can't build a sturdy romantic relationship if you skip the foundation of friendship, and we'd want him to be interested in more than our looks (or else he could have asked out our twin just as easily)."

"Dates go so much better. [It doesn't] feel like an interview."

"If a guy genuinely wants to be friends with me first, it makes me feel much better about the qualities I have aside from looks. If the guy asks too soon, then it does not feel like he knows me well enough to merit asking me out. I understand that guys and girls fall in love at different speeds, but paying attention to a woman's timing is of the utmost importance."

"My soon-to-be husband was patient for me and waited to ask me out, but in that time we developed a true, authentic friendship! We only hung out with friends and in groups and my oh my how it worked! Do fun things . . . Find out who they are as a person in a group of people and you'll fall in love organically!"

"I loved how my husband took the time to get to know me as a friend before even considering asking me on a date. That one year of friendship really helped to prevent assumptions about the other and prevented wasted time over not agreeing on core values."

Although building a foundation of friendship is good, don't wait forever. Consider what these three women said:

"If you are too calculated and wait too long, you lose the chance; you lose the moment."

"If you wait too long to ask me on a date then I'll assume I'm in the friend zone or you're leading me on."

"So many guys I know don't want to ask a girl they like out because they are afraid of rejection and so play it safe and keep themself in the friend zone. They say they want to wait to make sure they have a good friendship before asking the girl out. I think most guys forget that friendship can grow within an intentional dating relationship."

Perhaps this woman summed up the process best when she wrote:

"Start by building a friendship first. Treat her as your sister in Christ. Love her that way first, with no strings attached.

Once weeks or even months of a pure and holy friendship have been established, then if you have a strong desire to get to know her in a deeper way simply because you love who she is, then tell her exactly that. Don't go out with a girl out of curiosity. Know how you feel and what you want and she will be able to see it through you and if the desire is pure she will feel secure in that."

## Plan the date.

Of all the thirty-thousand-plus words of dating advice that I collected about what a woman wants, I'd have to say that the following words of wisdom were my favorite:

"DO NOT offer a Netflix and chill or take me to a sketchy warehouse or some weird lot and tell me about your felony record (speaking from experience)."

What we can glean from this story is that you should bring a woman to a fancy dinner if you plan to disclose your history of incarceration and the story behind your teardrop tattoo. All kidding aside, girls want you to plan the date. Perhaps the worst possible thing a man can utter to a woman when asked what they'll be doing is, "I don't know. What do *you* want to do?" Take a look at how insistent women were about this:

"Don't ask where she wants to go!!! Make a plan yourself!!"

"Just be decisive!! No girl wants to go on a date where the guy who is taking her on it has no idea what to do or where to go!"

"Most girls will be more attracted to the fact that he planned it himself rather than what the activity actually is."

"Put thought into and show the woman that you want some sort of future, not just a relationship that will die out. Show her you really care!"

"Show her you are capable of being a competent leader. Do not ask a girl out and then expect her to plan the date, make suggestions, or help you make decisions. If you get to know her likes and dislikes before planning and asking it's likely to impress her and it demonstrates your ability to be thoughtful and considerate."

"I know a lot of guys are trying to be considerate by inviting the girl into the planning process, but I'm way more impressed when a guy comes in with a plan. Even if it's not something I'd normally like or do, the thought and effort are what matter. I think working together to make plans for dates can come later once the couple has discerned they want to be in a relationship. In the beginning it's important to me that the guy shows he's willing to put in time and effort for me. I'm not saying he has to do something extravagant and expensive. The best dates I've been on are the simple ones where we got the chance to relax, have fun, and get to know each other."

Now that we've established the importance of planning a date, what should you plan? First off, remember that you're asking a woman *out*, you're not asking her *in*. One woman shared that a gentleman should invite her "somewhere public rather than asking to come over to his basement alone and watch a movie." Another hoped he would "Take her out to dinner during the day and not to his apartment."

So, if the plan is to take her out, where should you go? Women differed in their responses to this, but there were several common threads. One was that the purpose of a date is to get to know one another better. Therefore, many expressed that they would *not* want to go on a movie for a first date. One woman remarked, "Movie? No. Just no. If you go on a date with me, take me somewhere where we can talk and get to know each other—like to go get coffee."

While several women said they would like to be asked out for coffee, one noted, "Be a man when asking out a woman: Just say, 'I'd like to take you to dinner, are you available?' PS: Young guys, asking a girl out for coffee is what boys do—sends a message that you want 'try her out' before you spend the money on dinner."

However, this was an isolated response. One even noted, "I honestly don't really like to go to dinner on a first date because it makes it so formal." Another mentioned, "It can be as simple as getting coffee or lunch at Chick-fil-A."

One woman said, "Flowers are the way to a woman's heart!!" while another wrote: "Would NOT want . . . flowers."

Some said they would love to go to church on the first date, while others said they would not, "as I feel that is very intimate and can put undue pressure on the date."

One added, "Unless the girl is super religious (and you know she is the same denomination), don't ask to go to church for the first date." But another said, "If he asks if you want to pray with him, then he is doing things right! When the guy includes God in the date and in the relationship early and often the woman is always impressed and knows that this man isn't playing around."

So, how are you supposed to know what a woman wants? One answered:

"For me the best way to ask a girl out would be to first know her really well so you know what she really, really likes and customize that date according to her likes. There's nothing more charming than a guy who observes the little things we like."

In case you don't know her very well yet, here are a few universal principles:

Make it fun:

"Do something fun so you not only have time to talk but you can have fun together so the girl leaves thinking what a fun time she had."

"Doing something that both have never done helps to share something together—even if no one is a pro at it. Makes for memories!"

"First date ideas: drinks/coffee, festival (farmers market, street dance, live music), lunch, hockey/basketball/football/baseball game, rollerblading, some activity that allows you to talk but also gives pauses in case there is a lull in conversation."

Don't go overboard:

"First dates do not have to be extravagant. Usually the extravagance is what makes it awkward."

"It doesn't have to be glamorous. Just show the girl who you are."

"[Create a] casual plan and atmosphere that will not obligate us to spend hours together if it is not going well. So if it doesn't go well, you'd only stay for about an hour instead of four."

"It doesn't have to be super fancy or expensive. It's a chance to get to talk to your friend on a deeper level before getting into a relationship . . . But a first date as 'friends getting to know each other better' isn't the same as a first date as 'boyfriend and girlfriend.'"

"First dates should not be longer than 2½ hours."

In terms of the timing, be courteous and give her enough advance notice:

"The date should be within the week, but still give a few days to plan and prepare accordingly, like three days or so."

"If possible, have a date and time ready [when you ask]. Ironing out the details later isn't ideal, but it's not the end of the world either."

"Ask with a plan in mind for a set date and time, AT LEAST three days before said date. I hate the 'What are u up to right now? Wanna do something?' You want to make the girl feel important when you ask her out!"

"Offer to pick her up, but don't be weird about it if she says no."

"He should tell her in advance how she should dress (based on the date). Parts of it could be a surprise—which would be fun."

"I know lots of girls hate surprises, but I think it would mean even more if it was all kept secret!"

"Some girls like surprises and some really don't, so be open to telling her what you've planned if she needs that."

"Have a solid plan, but not so solid that 'we absolutely have to do this, this and this.'"

You'll notice the common desires in all the feedback above: If you put thought into it, make it fun, and create an environment in which you can get to know each other better, you've done well.

### Just ask her.

If you know who you want to ask, and where you'd like to take her on the date, all that remains is that you muster up the courage and ask! Before discussing *what* to say, it's important to know *where* to say it. Women were unanimous: They do not want to be asked out when they're with a group of people. They want to be asked in private, so they don't feel as if they're being put on the spot. Here's what three women shared:

"Make sure the guy asks the girl out when she is alone. Otherwise she might feel pressured to say yes because she doesn't want to embarrass the guy."

"I think the best way to be asked on a date would be in a private conversation in person. When guys try to ask girls out in a very public manner or a crowd, it almost makes the relationship feel like it's just for show, while over text could come off as just not being interested enough. What I mean by that is if a guy does not have the confidence and humility (by being open to rejection) to ask a girl out in person, then he could be lacking in that in other areas. Relationships thrive on communication, so when 'uncomfortable' or 'awkward' conversations come up, he might not be ready to engage in those conversations. For example, setting boundaries or apologizing. Keep it real."

"Not in front of a crowd of people or through someone else. It should be personal between the girl and the guy, it makes it all the more exciting and sweet."

As the last woman mentioned, the invitation needs to come from you, not from an intermediary. One woman stated:

"If you want to ask me out, ask ME out. I don't want to hear it from your friend or my friend. Be intentional. Be courageous. Our relationship is between us two, not the extra people around us."

What do you say when you approach her? Many men freeze before getting to this point because they don't know the exact words to say. Therefore, here's a litany of more than twenty ways that women said that they would like to be asked out. Some of the replies are similar, but providing such an exhaustive list will leave you no doubt as to what women hope to hear:

"I would want a guy to come up to me starting a conversation. I wouldn't want him focusing so much on how he feels about my physical appearance . . . Someone that genuinely wants to get to know me."

"I like when a guy comes to me, starts a simple conversation and uses it to ask me out . . . If he is my classmate, conversations can start with a class topic; if he's a friend in a social network, he can use one of my posts to start the conversation. These are just two examples."

"I'd like for him to begin with explaining why I caught his attention and then inviting me on a date somewhere."

"Ask in person, use her name (don't just start with 'Hey.' Address her)."

"Look me in the eye, and just be clear."

"When he asked, he held eye contact and though I could tell he was nervous, he was smiling and seemed genuinely excited at the thought of it happening."

"I want to take you out on a date, I was thinking we could go

____ and visit ____. Would that be of interest? When would you be available?"

"Just ask, 'Will you go on a date with me?' In person!"

"'There's tacos and margarita at this place . . . Wanna go and I'll buy you them!' If you get a NO I'll be shocked to my core."

"Being clear about your more-than-friendship interest is key. She can't give an honest answer if it's not clear what she's saying yes/no to."

"'I was wondering if you'd like to go on a date with me.' Any variation to that, fill it with affirmations with whatever, about how amazing I am, what your intentions are."

"I'd really like to get to know you better. Could I take you out on a date?"

"State your intentions: 'I'd like to take you out on a date because I want to get to know you and see if this could be something more.'"

"Hi, I've noticed you around and you seem to have a great personality. Can I take you out on a date?"

"I want to ask you out but I'm sure you'd want to get to know me first. Wanna get a cup of coffee so I can ask you on a real date after?"

"Say, 'Hey [insert name here], I really love spending time with you and I think you're a great girl. I'd love to get to know you more and I want to ask you if you'd give me the privilege of taking you out on a date.'"

"The best way I was ever asked on a date was this, 'Allison, being around you brings me instant joy. You are so interesting to me and I was wondering if you would allow me to take you on a date so that I can get to know you better?'"

"Hey, I think you're beautiful and I would like to know you more, would you like to go on a date with me?"

"I think you are really beautiful, and I have so much fun when I'm with you. Would you like to go on a date with me so we can get to know each other better?"

"I would love to go to dinner with you. Do you want to go on a date? I can pick you up at _____ and I'll take you to _____."

"Hey _____, I think you're really _____ (fun to be around, cool, kind, etc.) and I would love to get to know you more! Would you like to go on a date with me?"

"A simple 'I'd love to have dinner with you' would've swept me off my feet."

Besides clarity and simplicity, another common theme among the women's responses was that they appreciated a little bit of creativity:

"If he could think also a creative way to do it, I wouldn't turn him down. When I see a guy put thought and effort on something, I always will appreciate that."

"Ask the girl out in a way that makes her feel known, loved, pursued and wanted."

"A beautiful way for a guy to ask a girl on a date is something cute, quirky, something that shows that they aren't just going to do this for any girl."

"I think it would be really cool if a guy was in a bookstore and offered to buy me a book, instead of being in a bar and offering to buy me a drink."

"Coffee or dinner is fine, but if the girl loves to hike, for example, take the initiative to plan a fun activity you can enjoy together. Then say, 'I was hoping to do ____ and I'd like to do it with you as a date!'

"I walked into class early and he had flowers with a drawing of cartoon characters that said 'Wanna go on a date?' waiting for me. I felt totally flattered and it was the first time I said yes because I felt special. Every other guy used texting before him."

### Be brave.

No doubt, it can be nerve-wracking to ask a woman on a date. Perhaps you have countless hopes for where your relationship might lead, and you're not sure if the feelings are mutual. But there's only one way to find out: You have to face your fears. It's okay to experience feelings of nervousness, but it's not okay to let those feelings dictate your future. As one man said, "Courage is not the absence of fear, but rather the judgment that something else is more important than one's fear."[28] The real thing a man should fear is not rejection, but the possibility that the fear of rejection would paralyze him. Although you might be worried that a woman would detect your nervousness, you may be surprised to hear what they think about it:

"Dude, just be yourself—don't be afraid to be nervous (I find that adorable), just be yourself and be intentional. Don't do stuff over text—be bold! It shows you care."

"Honestly the fact that he wasn't cocky but ridiculously nervous was attractive. Let me tell you, best first date ever. He took me to the cutest little restaurant and gave me tickets to my favorite country artist who was going to be in the area a few weeks later. We've been together six years, married for three, and expecting our first baby in March."

Women know what's at stake when you ask them out. They know you're giving them the freedom to decline the offer, and they admire your decision to take a risk for them. Such courage in a man is appealing, whereas overconfidence is a turnoff:

"I can't imagine being with a guy who won't take any risk."

"Put yourself in a place where you are vulnerable to rejection. None of this 'We should hang out' or 'I'm gonna take you out,' or 'Let's go out.' No thank you. Ask a question that has a yes or no answer and that demands a response from the woman. It is attractive when men risk rejection."

"[Some men] don't want to face the possibility of being rejected and so they try to find some way to meet her without asking bravely and directly out . . . I really appreciate them being brave, it is so sweet."

"Seeing that a man is willing to put himself out there shows so much strength and servant-hearted intentions."

"It's awesome when the man takes the first step to get to know you more."

"I also need to know the guy is confident enough to want to pursue me, I want to see that he is in for the challenge."

"If you are interested in someone, make it clear. It gets messy when women AND men aren't clear as to what they want. I understand it can be hard to do this because of fear of rejection. But honestly, when a guy pursues a woman, it is so attractive!"

"We know that it takes courage because there is the possibility of rejection, we recognize it is difficult to ask us out because you have to become vulnerable with us, to step away from that 'masculine mantra' of the world and enter into a space of the unknown. We hold so much more respect for you men who do this because although you knew there was the possibility of rejection you thought we were worth it anyway!! That shows not that we are worthy because we are made worthy by God, but that we were worth the possible rejection to you."

This last comment shows that women appreciate a man who takes risks not simply because courage is a desirable masculine trait, but because risk taking shows how much you value her. One woman remarked, "It makes you feel loved, especially when someone takes his time to plan a date, find the courage to ask a girl out in person, and to have a good intention on dating."

When a woman sees a man's confidence combined with his willingness to risk rejection, she becomes more likely to accept his invitation:

"Chances are high the girl will say yes if you're friends who hang out often and enjoy each other's company. Being clear is extremely attractive and emits confidence."

"My own personal rule is that first dates can never hurt (unless I already know I don't want to be with that person)."

"Even if the guy is really nervous when asking in person and stumbling and having a hard time, he needs to know that asking in person is still WAY better than asking over text and shows that he cares enough to put himself out there. It shows that he's strong which, spoiler alert: Women want strong men to lead them. The guy has to take the initiative and show he is able to lead. Also, if the woman he is asking is a mature and virtuous woman she will most likely say yes to one date."

"Confidence is a great thing but be careful not to come off as if you're 'doing her a favor' by taking her out. Most of all, don't be afraid to be excited! If you're feeling triumphant about an accepted invitation, it's ok to show it! It's actually very charming when men show their genuine reactions, so there's no need to 'play it cool.'"

If, after reading all of the above counsel from women, you're still unsure of how to begin, try this: Begin by having more casual conversations with women you don't know well, and perhaps ones you're not even attracted to. You'll feel less pressure because there's no opportunity for rejection when there is no invitation being offered. Obviously, you want to avoid flirting with these women or leading them on in any way. Integrity is key. As you develop more social experience with women, you'll feel more confident in interacting with ones who might be potential dates. But in the end, keep in mind that a woman will be more flattered by the man who bravely overcomes his nervousness than she will be by the man who thinks he's irresistible.

### Practice dating etiquette.

One woman noted that if you follow the steps above, "I promise this would get our attention!" So, presuming you planned the date and she said yes, how does a woman hope you'll act during the date? Here are some pointers from women regarding the manners they hope to find in you:

"If you're coming to pick me up for a date, come to my door. Don't send me a text that you're outside."

"Walk to the front door. Ring the doorbell, don't text from the car."

"If you're not man enough to meet my dad, you're not man enough to meet me, and if you're too lazy to come to the door I'm too lazy to come to the car."

"Don't walk through a door and let the door 'hit' the girl behind you."

"Open her door for her, pick her up, pay for her meal."

"Open the door not only for her, but the people behind you as well."

"Pull out her chair."

"Don't feel confused about paying. You are asking her out, you should be the one paying."

"It's nice to be told that I don't have to worry about bringing my wallet because it's a date and he's the man."

"Assume that you'll be paying for the date, do not expect that from her. But again, if she insists on paying, don't be weird about it."

"Ask the person questions and not just initial ones but follow up to show that you are really listening. A guy would get major points for listening well."

"No lame or mean or over-flirty jokes on a date."

"Do not call every girl you meet babe, hon, sweetie, or anything like this. It's creepy."

"Don't call girls hot or anything like that, as this shows you don't value her."

"GENTLE, I'm not your bro."

"It's also a huge plus when a guy isn't on his phone the whole time you're with him!"

"Don't talk about marriage on the first date."

"Be intentional and lead, not like a chauvinist but gently and lovingly. Invite us to pray with you, open the door for us, etc. Treat us with dignity and respect and for the love of God, be normal and make us laugh!"

One of the worst things a man can possibly do at the end of a date is to make a woman feel as if she owes him something for the time they've spent together. They owe each other a thank you, and that's it. Therefore, to conclude your date in a respectful way, consider the feedback from these women:

"Don't expect an intimate kiss on the first date."

"He needs to have the mind-set of protecting her, not pushing her."

"Most of my first dates ended in a hug, which I always found very sweet (no creepy hugs though).

"Kindly do not go on a date with an expectation of 'getting something.' Just go on a date to spend time with each other."

"If he likes you, he should say it, and ask you out again. Texting seems okay for following up, but I much prefer calling and leaving voicemails."

"Do not ask about there being a second date until after the first date."

All of this can be summarized with one simple reflection: Imagine that the date goes as well as you could have ever hoped. As time goes on, you both grow in appreciation and love for each other, and one day become husband and wife. Then, God blesses you with a wonderful daughter who steals your heart and looks just like your bride. Your little princess grows up and becomes a stunningly beautiful young woman . . . and then you get a knock at the door and it's her date. Treat her mom tonight like you would want that gentleman to treat your daughter two decades from now.

### You're not dating because you took her on a date.

One reason why men don't ask women out—especially in smaller social circles—is that they fear the woman will assume that the date is a prelude to certain commitment. He fears that if he asks one woman out this week and another three weeks from now, he'll be viewed as a player. So, he asks no one out and the women are left to form dating bereavement groups, bemoaning the fact that guys don't have the guts to ask anyone out. How do we break this frustrating cycle?

A few things are needed. For one, when a man asks a woman on a date, he needs to explain clearly that this is an opportunity for them to get to know one another better. They're not committing to each other yet. They're agreeing to explore the possibility of dating. A date doesn't make you a boyfriend. Becoming physical with a woman doesn't make her your girlfriend. Spending lots of time with her doesn't mean that the two of you have somehow become "official."

You become a boyfriend by asking a woman if she will be your girlfriend. That's the only proper route. It's a separate decision and requires just as much clarity as when you asked her on a date. Another step of decisiveness and clarity will be required if you propose to her one day, and the same is true on the day you marry. At every stage, a clear choice is made. Don't *slide* from one stage to the next; *decide*.

Here's what some women had to say about the distinction between a date and being in a committed relationship:

"A date is meant to get to know someone. Some guys need to understand that you're not automatically boyfriend and girlfriend. That's why not many people typically ask someone specifically to go on a date."

"Intentions should be 100% clear by the end of the third date, because it takes a couple to figure out how you feel. If you're not sure by the fourth date, it's probably a no."

"Dating is a process of intentionally getting to know someone and see if you're compatible on a whole variety of different levels (values, personalities, interests, etc.). I think a lot of heartache would be spared both for men and for women if they entered into each date with this mind-set. And if it's only a couple dates, fine! It's not a breakup. 'Intentionality' does not equate to 'This is it! I love you. We're in a relationship.'"

"Asking a girl on a date doesn't mean you're asking her to be your girlfriend or that she is 'yours.' It just means you're getting to know them better; you could be on a date with one girl one day and another the next week if the first wasn't for you."

"You aren't committed to a relationship with that person, you've only been on one date."

"More than three dates and I'd say you're going to have to become more committed soon if it's still being pursued."

"My husband was always 100% clear about our relationship. I never had to play the guessing game with him (Does he like me? Am I his girlfriend? What are we doing?). I loved how secure I felt in that. Another thing he did was write me letters and actually mail them to my house. Who does that anymore? None of the guys I dated before . . . and none of them are my husband."

"My now-fiancé would go scope out date locations days before asking me to go on a particular date. He went to the lake where he wanted to ask me to be his girlfriend several days in a row to make sure he had the timing of the sunset just right."

Several women also expressed that it's important a man not get ahead of himself regarding his future plans with her:

"Also DO NOT tell me you want to marry me, that you feel called to marry me. Discernment is done WITH the person not for or about them before you even date. Sure, say you want to see if we're called to marriage, awesome because I'm not dating you for fun. It's intentional but it's not predestined."

"Most people think discernment is before you even date them like, uhm, you discern with the person."

"Just because you go on a couple dates doesn't mean you're going to marry that person. Dates are not covenants."

"Do not start with 'Will you discern marriage with me?' Though the purpose of dating is to find your spouse this is way too much pressure to put on someone you just asked out, especially if you are not that close."

"The worst a guy can do is pin everything on God: 'I've been discerning/praying about this, and I think God wants me to ask you out . . .' I'm all for a praying man, but when someone sounds like they have the monopoly on God's will, it's a red flag."

### When she says no.

Although the above counsel is helpful, it's not a guaranteed recipe for success. For any number of reasons, she may decline your invitation for a date. If she offers a reason why she can't go (for example, she has plans to rearrange her sock drawer that month), you're looking at one of two possibilities: Either she's not interested, or she genuinely has a schedule conflict. How do you know which is the case? Easy: If she's interested, she'll propose a different time that works for her. If she doesn't, then you have your answer.

If the woman declines your invitation for a date, Paul J. Kim suggests you look on the bright side: "There are billions of other women in the world, and you've just narrowed down the search for your future spouse."[29] In other words, asking a woman out is a win-win situation. Either you end up with a date, or you end up with clarity. Either way, it's better than being alone and unsure.

Here's what women had to say about times when they had to turn down a date:

"Don't take a 'no' personally. Sometimes it's just not a good fit or the girl isn't in a place where she wants to date."

"If she's says she can't make it that day, come up with another day/time. She will either accept or decline and you will know if you should keep pursuing or not."

"Also, be man enough to accept rejection, don't keep asking every few days to see if I've changed my mind."

"It would also be great that he at least act confident enough in himself so that she can say 'no' freely and not feel an obligation to accept something she doesn't want to in order to spare his feelings."

"If he is rejected, he should not mope about it too much, or pressure her."

"Persistence is NOT always key. Respect her boundaries."

"Respect her decision. A negative reaction to a woman declining your invitation just gives her reassurance she made the right choice."

"If a girl turns you down for some reason though, do NOT backtrack and be like 'Haha, yeah I wasn't really looking to date anyway,' or 'Haha, that wasn't serious.' Stick to being clear and intentional, regardless of her response."

## No ghosting.

After a date, some men who are not interested in pursuing the woman any further choose to become invisible and drop off the face of the earth. Otherwise known as "ghosting," this is perhaps is one of the most bothersome and dismissive things a man can do to a woman at any stage of their relationship. I presume many of these men have good intentions, not wanting to hurt the woman's feelings. However, leaving her in the dark is both hurtful and confusing. She's left to ponder various scenarios of what she did wrong, why she's not alluring enough, or why the man lost interest. Regardless of how sincere a man's intentions might be, it's a cowardly thing to do.

To be honest, I've done it more than once. In seventh grade, my girlfriend broke up with me because I forgot I was dating her. One would hope that I would have changed by the time I was in college, but I remember doing it there as well.

I met a young woman, felt a strong initial attraction toward her, took her to a dance and went on a few quasi-dates, and then lost interest and moved on without a single conversation. Looking back, I can only imagine how confused she must have felt.

So, what's the honorable thing for a man to do if he isn't interested in taking the relationship any further? Step one is to realize that it's easy for a man to be brave, confident, sincere, and honest if it increases his chances of a woman saying yes to a first date. But such a man's character is better measured by how he handles the end of a relationship. Is he willing to be brave, confident, sincere, and honest for *her* sake? In asking a woman out, a man has asked for a certain responsibility with her heart. He needs to follow through with this responsibility until the end. When he ghosts, he drops it.

Because it can be tricky to end a relationship tactfully, I surveyed hundreds of additional women about how they would want a man to communicate that he's not interested in taking things any further. Once again, clarity and sincerity were key. One of the first things women noted was the widespread problem of ghosting, and how much it hurt them:

"An ending should be just as intentional and clear as initiating our first date. Start strong, guys! Every time I have been ghosted, it was with a guy [who] also was not clear if this was a date or not."

"Be honest. Maybe the girl feels the same way and then you just made a really good friend! When you ghost someone, you lose that chance [of] making a friendship."

"If it turns out you are not interested or don't want to continue the relationship or conversation, just say so . . . Don't leave us hanging!"

"When they become invisible, then you feel invisible. You don't matter enough to be present to them."

"Ghosting is an epidemic of immaturity in men."

"Being truthful does not equate to being ruthless and insensitive to the other's feelings . . . If anything, that's what ghosting is."

"We just want the respect of them being honest. If you don't want to continue the relationship, simply say so and why for closure. That can be respected, where ghosting is never okay."

"I'd rather be told that his intentions and interests have changed rather than sitting in a nebulous cloud of confusion and questions."

"Don't make her figure it out for herself based on your lack of communication. It can cause a wound that can affect future relationships."

"It's basically sending the message that you don't respect someone as a human being enough to have a crucial (sometimes hard) and honest conversation with them about how you're feeling. And honestly, if you're not mature enough to talk about your feelings (or lack thereof), then maybe you're not ready for a relationship whatsoever."

If ghosting is the wrong way to conclude a relationship, then what's the right way to go about it? I asked the women this question and discovered that just as different women preferred to be asked out in different ways, the same was true of breaking up or not moving forward toward a relationship. Some wanted to know exactly went wrong. For example:

"If you want someone to learn something from the relationship, be honest but kind and say, 'This is what didn't work for me.' If every guy I've been ghosted by did that I would have much clearer knowledge of what I need to work on and change about what I'm doing in my effort to find my soulmate."

However, a number of other women preferred not to know too many details as to why he lost interest:

"Whatever you say, DO NOT pinpoint any specific characteristic that you dislike in her, or would like in someone but don't see in her; it's not necessary or kind and won't change the outcome so just don't."

"Be honest but not too honest. I don't need to hear all the bad things about me or why we wouldn't work. I just want to know how you feel and I want honesty."

"Do it in a way that won't lead the girl to think that she wasn't enough for him."

"Say it in a loving way that won't make girls feel 'unworthy.'"

"Honesty, however, doesn't mean he has to say EVERY-THING he thinks about her. If the reason for the rejection is objective, yes, it's good that he tells her (like, if he wants to have a family and she doesn't, or if he wants to have chaste relationship and she doesn't, and so on). But if he just sees that he doesn't like her for subjective matters (like they don't have that much in common, or her personality doesn't match his, or if he thinks she is not ____ enough, and so on) he doesn't have to tell her the defects that makes him not be interested in her."

If women differ in how they want men to express their lack of interest, is there really any good way to let a woman go? There is. Just as a man should ask a woman out in person—with courage and honesty—the same should be true of a breakup. Earlier in this chapter, I provided a list of examples of how a man might ask a woman out. In case the relationship doesn't go the way you had hoped, here's how women said men could respectfully end a relationship:

"I am so grateful for the guy who called me the day after the first date to say he had a great time, really enjoyed our conversation, and just wanted to be up front with me rather than lead me on that he didn't really see it going anywhere . . . I was so thankful for how he handled this!

"There is no easy way to end a relationship. But please have an actual conversation, texting isn't respectful and trivial-izes the relationship."

"If it's the early stages of a relationship a phone call seems to be okay, but if you've been in a relationship for a while it's gotta be face-to-face."

"Men should be clear. Men are called to represent Christ . . . and the Word says that God is not the author of confusion."

"If they haven't dated yet but are still in the 'talking' phase and he isn't sure about her feelings towards him, I feel like it's okay for him to slowly back off as long as he's very clear in his intentions—not flirting or being overly friendly, just distancing himself. If you've spent a lot of time together and she clearly has feelings, he needs to be more clear and intentional, and a conversation needs to be had."

"My friend went on a second date with a guy and she wasn't into him anymore. She was afraid she would have to do the 'breaking up.' But the day after their second date, he sent her a text that basically complimented her, he told her what he liked about her, like her passion and her care and concern for other people, etc. Then he said he enjoyed the time he spent with her but knew he wasn't right for her, and hoped she would find someone who was right for her because she deserved to be with that perfect person. He closed with another compliment. It was sincere and heartfelt, and made his feelings/ intentions clear, while also making her feel good."

"Don't put God in the mix. It hurts when they say, 'God made me do this.'"

What exactly should the man say? Here are several examples various women offered:

"I'm no longer interested in pursuing this any further and I wish you all the best with the future."

"I've had a really great time getting to know you. I just don't think I'm interested in a romantic relationship with you."

"As a man I want to guard you heart and be honest and up front with you and I just want to let you know that I don't have a desire to move things forward."

"It has been great to know you better but I prefer to stop dating you because I know now that I'm not meant to be in a relationship with you. You are a great person and the right guy will be blessed to have you. I don't want to waste your time or play with your feelings, [so] I have to be honest with you. Thank you for the opportunity."

"I don't feel that we are a good match."

"I've appreciated the time we've spent together, and you have amazing qualities, but it helped me see that we may not be the best fit. I wanted to tell you this now so that we can both move on to find our best fits."

"I really admire you as a person and I would still like to be friends, but I do not see this relationship going anywhere romantically."

When should you have this conversation? Immediately:

"I would want him to tell me as soon as possible so as not to waste my time and his."

"At the end of the date, don't just leave on vague terms! [If you enjoyed it,] tell her you had a great time with her and that you would like to do it again. If you didn't enjoy the date, make sure you tell her very soon that you aren't interested in a romantic relationship. Please don't just leave her in the dark! She will appreciate the clear and timely communication so much, especially if you do it sooner rather than later."

"As soon as he knows he isn't interested I think he should say something to me face-to-face. Save me a heartbreak and confusion. I'd rather know it's not working out than growing attached to someone who has moved on."

"It'll hurt either way, but we'll get over it. Best to state your feelings up front. Time is precious."

"Let me know asap when you sense it's not going to work. Let me know if you're certain it's not going to work or if there is potential that we can talk through, pray through. I think if I heard the problem expressed in this manner, I could move on easier."

"Honesty is best, and as soon as he starts feeling confused if he should still pursue her or not, he should let her know the next time he sees her. Plan a hangout and make sure she knows it's not a date. And just hold a conversation with her and be real and truthful, but do so gently."

"Please don't take more than a week to decide what you want if you're doubting all of a sudden, cause your girl needs to keep moving forward with or without you. Please tell her as soon as you know (and if you honestly don't have the guts to tell her, you shouldn't be dating in the first place)."

One reason why men often avoid these tough conversations is because they don't want to hurt the woman's feelings. Although they may have lost interest in pursuing the relationship, they still care about the woman and want to avoid feeling guilty about causing her pain. But listen to what the women said about this:

"Being rejected hurts, but being ghosted hurts more because it shows me that I am not worthy enough to warrant an explanation for how you are feeling. Be respectful and let a girl know as soon as you are aware that you are not interested, as this leaves a girl still feeling dignified. Confrontation is always awkward, but it is also a great sign of maturity and strength."

"Be honest if you are no longer interested in a relationship and if she asks for clarity never refuse her. It is respectful of her personhood and it helps her guard her heart. If you never give her clarity, she will likely continue hoping you may return. So, if you have no intention of returning, just say so. Honesty doesn't hurt as bad as being misled."

"Yes, it will sting, but in the long run its better for her than crying and pondering what she did wrong and why the guy isn't getting back to her."

"She may still cry or be heartbroken. But you will be implicitly telling her, 'You're not the one for me, but that doesn't mean you're not worth being loved.' That's being a real gentleman."

"Yeah it hurts, but at least no more time will be wasted, and she can invest it in someone who is invested in her. There is nothing wrong with not liking someone because we can't all marry each other."

"It will hurt but it's better to end it there, then live with the pain of leaving without closure."

"Just be clear! Don't be a coward! We are strong! We can handle the truth. We don't need you to try and protect us; actually we just need you to be honest with us!"

A man should not wait until he is leaving a relationship to think about how he can minimize the pain of a breakup. It's something he should consider before he even enters one. Breakups tend to be less traumatic when the couple takes their time, both physically and emotionally in the relationship. Furthermore, when dating relationships are pure, couples often remain friends afterward. It's a smoother landing. On the other hand, when unmarried couples become sexually intimate, their breakups often feel like an emotional divorce. Therefore, pace yourself. As one woman noted:

"Do everything in your power to not let the flow of your relationship with her be rushed. Take your time and be friends first! Then there is no reason for ghosting at all. Ghosting mostly happens when the relationship develops too fast and you feel the need to stomp on the brakes."

When the time comes to end a relationship, be lovingly decisive. Commit to your breakup. In other words, don't flounder in your decision. This will only cause more hurt. Consider what the following women wrote:

"Be consistent!! If you say you're not interested, don't go back on your word with your actions. Give the friendship space to figure out where to go from there, if anywhere."

"Tell them exactly how you're feeling and don't give any false hope."

"I'm honest with guys if I'm not interested because I don't want them hung up on someone [who] isn't interested. DONT KEEP THEM AS MAYBES! They are a yes or a no. You don't get to leave a girl holding on to a 'maybe one day.' Be present, be bold, and man up."

"Don't then pop back in when it's convenient for you and use me as your 'emotional fidget spinner,' as my friend put it, whenever you're bored."

"You should only say that you 'want to be friends' if you really are open to a casual friendship. If that would be too awkward or you're not interested in her platonically, then don't pretend you are. Leading people on in friendships is a thing, too."

## How NOT to Date

The above counsel might feel like a lot to remember. To make it easier to recall, let's flip it all backward. Below is the perfect summary of how not to date a woman:

Step one is to incessantly flirt with her, while keeping her in the friend zone. This strategy offers you two benefits: First, it gives her the opportunity to ask you out, which is the safest route. You're a modern man, liberated from the confines of binary gender stereotyping. Also, it creates romantic tension because she has no idea what you're thinking. This is a good time to show her you're a true gentleman by asking for revealing pictures. That way, you can get to know her on a more personal level.

If she drags her feet and doesn't ask you out after one or two years, then it's time to act decisively. Have your friend text her on your behalf and ask for her social media information, since you couldn't find her on your favorite dating app. If she says no, be persistent. A little cockiness goes a long way. Text her and let her know you think she's "hot," call her "Lil mama," and ask if she wants to "hang out" or chill at your place. After all, girls love dark basements, old couches, and gaming. #Romance.

If persistence and poutiness don't do the trick, go public and ask her in the presence of multiple people. Women love being put on the spot like that. Whatever you do, don't say the word "date." That's way too clear. It could mean rejection for you, and that's not a risk you want to take. Your feelings might get hurt! Spare your ego. It's also smart to keep her guessing what your intentions really are, because this makes you a man of mystery.

When she asks what the plan is, avoid eye contact and mumble, "I dunno. What do you wanna do?" Indecisiveness is irresistible. When you pick her up for the date—um, I mean to *hang out*—just text her "HERE" (all caps) to let her know that you've arrived, since she's capable of walking unassisted to your uncleaned vehicle. If the car smells, just spritz a generous amount of masculine-smelling body spray in the car beforehand (and on yourself, for good measure) to neutralize any odor. No need to open doors for her, because you don't want to offend her by being too patriarchal. Go to a movie, so you can get to know her better while sitting in silence for two hours. When the dinner bill arrives, stare at with wide eyes, slide it over to her, and say, "Whoa, I wouldn't pay that much if I were you!" Just kidding, that's rude. Just split the dinner bill, because you're already paying for the gas.

Before the evening comes to a close, make sure to gather all her social media account information so that you can get to know her even better without having to call her. When the night ends and you've invested all of this effort, you deserve a payoff. Attempt to enter her dwelling and behave in a petulant manner if she doesn't express her profound gratitude with a prolonged passionate kiss. If you're not sure if you ever want to see her again, just fade into oblivion without communicating your intentions moving forward. You wouldn't want to bother her with clarity when she would much rather spend the next several weeks overthinking the matter with her girlfriends. Girls bond like that, so you're doing her a favor by giving them fodder for their speculative conversations.

If all of this doesn't work, here's one final idea: Put down your dumb phone and stop hiding behind a screen. Look a girl in the eyes and ask her on a *date*. Face the fear of rejection like a man because a woman is worth it.

# 4

# DATE YOUR SOULMATE

My college girlfriend and I sat on a bench under the shade of a grove of trees on campus, having a long conversation as our two-year relationship was coming to a close. Things were ending on good terms, but it was clear that it was time for us to move on. During the conversation, she expressed to me with kindness that it always bothered her that I never asked her out.

I sat in silent bewilderment after she said this, mulling over the past few years we had spent together, mentally fact-checking her statement. She was right . . . I forgot to do that. I then realized that I did the same thing with the two women I dated before her. I had dated a total of three women over a span of five years in college, with no idea as to when I started dating any of them! And if I didn't know when we began dating, it's safe to assume that they had no idea either! However, in one of the relationships, we even looked at wedding rings together. In each case, the friendships gradually morphed into dating relationships without me ever asking any of these women if we could become official.

At the time, I saw this as a natural way to enter a relationship: You meet a girl, gradually spend time with her in a group setting, then more time alone, and eventually . . . *voila!* It's obvious to everyone in the world (except perhaps her) that you're dating. There's no risk of rejection because there's no question being asked. There's no clear line of demarcation between friends and more than friends. Ask any woman, and they'll tell you: This is not the way to go. It's about as manly as texting a woman to ask if she wants to "hang out."

In each of these relationships, I wasn't trying to avoid commitment. My intentions were sincere and my interest in each of them was genuine. But it shocked me that I could be so blind to something that they desired. It's safe to assume that I'm not the only one who has done this. Our culture of male indecisiveness is taking its toll on women, and they're tired of pretending to be the girlfriend of a man who never asks to be a boyfriend.

Therefore, if a man has done his work of discernment and pursued a woman with sincerity, what remains is for him to commit to her with clarity. In the previous chapter, women raved about how desirable it was for a man to initiate dates with clarity, so that she doesn't need to wonder what he's asking of her. The same clarity is appropriate when it's time to enter into a committed dating relationship.

When a man extends a clear invitation to a woman for the two of them to enter an exclusive dating relationship, he is honoring her once again with the freedom to choose. He's giving her the chance to decide what they are, and what they are not. Should she say yes, his work is not finished. One of the greatest challenges of dating will be to sustain this clarity. What they *are* is dating. What they are *not* is married (emotionally, physically, or spiritually).

## Sexual Honesty

Sending mixed signals to the opposite sex isn't just a guy problem. Men and women alike are guilty of leading the other on, ghosting, or assuming commitment exists when it doesn't. Without clarity, dating is complicated. Just as this is true on an emotional level, it's also true on a physical one. When two people who aren't dating begin to express physical affection, their hearts assume that they are dating. In the same way, when dating couples begin to express sexual affection, they begin to feel married.

Unbeknownst to men, this is a frightening situation for unmarried women. This is because the woman does not simply give her body during sex; more often than not, she gives herself. But if she's giving her body and heart to a man who is not her husband, it may feel like she's hang-gliding a thousand feet above earth without a parachute. She can only hope that everything will work out. If something malfunctions, it will be a long drop. Because she doesn't enjoy the security of a wife, she fears what might happen if she becomes pregnant or if he loses interest.

Meanwhile, on the other side of the relationship, the opposite effect tends to happen. When a man enjoys the marital privilege without marital responsibility, he often loses any sense of urgency to move the relationship forward. This often causes relationships to stall out and coast in neutral for years on end. He may think, "Why complicate things by getting married? If I can enjoy the pleasures of marriage without its demands, what's the rush?"

Contrary to popular belief, the problem with sexual intimacy prior to marriage isn't that the couple is going "too far." If anything, they're not going far enough. When a man truly loves a woman, he doesn't just give her his body. He gives her his last name, his address, his bank account, his fatherhood, and his future. A woman is worth nothing less.

Consider the language of sex: The bodies are saying, "I am entirely yours." But if the two are unmarried, this is untrue. This is why the total gift of the body (sex) should correspond with the total gift of the person (marriage). When this happens, and spouses consummate their love, they are speaking the truth in their bodies. They're renewing their wedding vows in the flesh.

The nature of the sexual act demands permanence. Aside from the emotional bond, making love makes babies. The child is permanent and eternal, like the love a man should have for the woman to whom he makes love. Life and love are inseparable. No matter how hard our culture may try, sex cannot be separated from fatherhood. When we try to divorce the two, we end up losing respect for women, ourselves, and sex itself. Pregnancy becomes a risk rather than a blessing. Fatherhood becomes a fear instead of a gift. Also, the woman is no longer viewed as a person or a potential mother. In our desire to receive pleasure isolated from complete responsibility, sex becomes lifeless.

Some may ask, "Why would God give us all these desires if we're not supposed to act on them?" This is a fair question.

When an army sends troops into battle, it first trains them. Otherwise, imagine the chaos. Imagine if soldiers were simply given tanks and told to try their best. They would trample innocent civilians, accidentally fire rounds at friendly targets, and cause more harm than good. In the same way, our sexual urge has the power for both life and destruction, and every boy who wishes to become a man must learn to discipline his desires by using his interior strength. If he does not, he may leave a trail of damaged and discarded women in his wake.

Consider these years of intense temptations as a preparation and training for the demands of real love. You may know that when the United States military selects its elite soldiers (Navy Seals, Green Berets, Army Rangers, etc.), it must sift through thousands of men in order to find the few who are capable of the completing the most grueling missions. So, the military subjects all applicants to torturous testing. For example, the Navy Seals face "hell week." During the five-day period, the troops will burn between five thousand and seven thousand calories per day. The candidates will swim for miles, run obstacle courses repeatedly, carry inflatable boats through frigid waters, and so on, with about an hour of sleep per day. Broken bones and torn ligaments are not uncommon, and physicians examine the men at least once a day to make certain that no lives are lost. Those who persevere to the end earn the title of Navy Seal and are given great responsibilities to ensure our country's safety.

One might feel that such testing is cruel or extreme, but we sleep in peace knowing that such soldiers exist. Over 1500 years ago the Athenian general Thucydides wrote, "We must remember that one man is much the same as another, and that he is best who is trained in the severest school."[30] Therefore, the military puts men into the fire in order to reveal their value. When these troops face the distress of battle, it will be nothing new. They will have trained themselves for the hardships.

Similarly, Karol Wojtyła remarked, "Love must be tested like gold in the fire. Only small love disintegrates in the fire of trials; great love is purified and grows more ardent. Real purity enables us to love."[31] Although resisting temptations is difficult, it is precisely this difficulty that builds virtue. In weightlifting, one of the necessary factors in building muscle is "time under tension." The same is true of the moral life: Resistance builds a man into one.

When a man practices self-restraint prior to marriage, he trains himself in faithfulness. If he can resist temptations with the woman he loves more than life itself, he will be well prepared to resist temptations with other women once he's married. If seasons of abstinence are required of him within marriage, he'll be ready for the sacrifice. This is serious marriage preparation.

Some men might wonder if they'll be unprepared for marital intimacy if they don't experience it beforehand. But think about it: What do women truly want? Are they on a quest to find the man with the most extensive sexual history? Is sexual "experience" anywhere on their list of desirable attributes in a partner? It's not. A man will make love as he loves. If he is selfless, patient, caring, and attentive, all of these things will translate into the bedroom. The same is true if he is self-absorbed, impatient, aggressive, and inattentive.

Sexual desires are healthy and normal, but if a man doesn't learn to control his desires, his passions will control him. When this happens, the good of the relationship is no longer his first concern. But when a man is able to resist this aggressive appetite in order to sacrifice for love of the woman, he becomes, in the truest sense, a gentleman.

Granted, there's much more that goes into building a solid dating relationship than the one virtue of chastity. It would be myopic to think that this is the only necessary ingredient. However, the presence of this virtue is often a good indication of the overall health of a relationship, because it requires many of the same virtues that keep love thriving, such as patience, sacrifice, and selflessness.

## Guard Your Love

Maintaining a pure relationship is obviously easier said than done. But if you follow the following ten strategies, you'll discover that such a lifestyle isn't simply possible, it's liberating.

### Don't get emotionally married.

The desire for union is part of love. Couples yearn for closeness not only emotionally, but physically. Especially in the case of a woman, her body wants to go where her heart goes. But if there are no emotional boundaries within the relationship, physical boundaries aren't likely to last.

Therefore, pace yourselves. Maintain interests and friendships outside of the relationship. Allow it to breathe. Don't feel the need to pour out all your deepest, darkest secrets to one another while talking on the phone nightly for hours. Give the relationship time and space to grow.

### Never wait for her to say no.

Many men assume that males are the only ones with strong sexual desires. They may think, "Sure, women have temptations. But not like us. Therefore, it's the woman's job to decide when we need to draw the line. I'm a good guy, and I'll totally respect her when she says no." But consider how disrespectful this is to women. During physical intimacy, she may be thinking, "I enjoy this, but I'm starting to feel like I'm compromising my morals. How am I supposed to stop without getting him upset? I don't want to hurt his feelings. Maybe he'll stop, so I don't have to."

To avoid this, don't be the "good guy" who assumes he's noble for "respecting" a woman when she finally tells him to stop. No man gets points for *not* forcing a woman to do something against her will. That's a man's duty, not a sign of his moral quality. If a woman ever has to say no to you physically, you've already gone too far.

Living a chaste life requires a man to examine the motives and the subtle movements within his heart. By leading a woman closer to heaven or away from it, he demonstrates his real intentions.

### Don't rationalize lust.

Some men assume that they are entitled to sexual intimacy because their feelings are so genuine and intense. They might presume to know the future because they've never felt so close to a woman in the past. As a result, they begin justifying the expression of marital affection before marital commitment. They think: "It's not a big deal if we do this, because we've already done that." Or, "We've already done it once. What's the big deal if it happens again?" Or, "It's not like we just met. We've been together for years."

Have you ever noticed that if you're doing something good, you never make justifications for it? You'll never feed the homeless and think to yourself, "Well, at least I'm not robbing a bank." When your acts are good, your conscience is at rest. Meanwhile, when we compromise, we look for a reason to excuse ourselves.

### Do it for love.

If a man is unable to practice such self-control with his girlfriend, he should not assume it is because his love for her is so great. Rather, as one Orthodox theologian remarked, "A weakened form of eros desires beauty without the cross."[32] Ruminate on the wisdom of his insight: When we sin, it is not because our desires are too strong. Rather, they're too weak. When a man truly loves a woman, he will go to any lengths to guard the goodness of their love.

When he drops his guard and lust begins to pollute a couple's love, the woman is not the only one who is impacted. Men sometimes grow listless and bored with the relationship and even themselves. They may think "I don't even want to be around myself when I'm with her. I don't respect myself. But since I can't leave me, I'll leave her." One young man emailed me and noted, "Looking back I can see we stopped learning about each other the moment the sex started."

Granted, this isn't always the case. Some men claim that the physical intimacy has only served to strengthen their bond. What they often don't consider is that they may be strengthening their bond with someone else's future wife. For this reason, abstinence is an expression of love even to those we have yet to meet. One woman emailed me and shared a letter she had written to her future husband, about her desire to wait for him. In it, she wrote:

"For now, love means waiting, as patiently as I can, until me, you, and all the people we love are ready for us. It means not wasting my time with people I know are not you, and hoping against all hope that when we are ready, we will meet, and finally get to experience the whirlwind that is each other, and that we will be able to experience that for the rest of our lives, together. So for now I will wait, as hard as it may be, and love you in a million little ways, and endlessly fall in love with the man I don't know, the man that is you."

## Avoid the occasion.

Forest fires that devastate countless acres often begin with a small match or spark. In the same way, the biggest mistakes often begin with the smallest compromises. Therefore, to guard purity, avoid the places and situations that are likely to cause temptation.

Neuroscientists from the University of Cambridge discovered that "'precommitment'—voluntarily restricting one's access to temptation—is more effective at promoting self-control than willpower."[33] Therefore, succeeding at chastity isn't simply about being strong in the presence of temptation; it's more about being humble enough to avoid the allure of sin altogether.

Although strategies to avoid temptation are important and helpful, as Eric Metaxas said, "Being a Christian is less about cautiously avoiding sin than about courageously and actively doing God's will."[34]

## Practice male modesty.

The word "modesty" never seems to apply to men. For whatever reason, modesty is typically regarded as something women ought to be concerned about so they don't "cause" us to sin. The notion of male modesty is puzzling and even amusing. What does it mean? Do we need to throw away all of our European-style bathing suits? Do we need to stop wearing oversized jeans with our underwear protruding from our backsides? For most of us, these aren't viable wardrobe options, much less temptations.

To understand modesty, we need to step away from the narrow understanding of modesty as it pertains to clothing only. Yes, we ought to avoid styles of clothing that might be an occasion of sin for others. Personally, I'm not sure what type of garb I would need to don in order to incline anyone to sin. Regardless, a man can practice modesty in countless other ways, including his intentions and in the way he dances with women and interacts with them. He ought to practice modesty even when women are nowhere around, by the way he speaks. Modesty doesn't make him womanly. If anything, it makes him more of a man. It requires him to defend the dignity of women, even at the expense of his own social status.

### Go to the source.

Hundreds of years ago, there was a young man who struggled mightily in his battles with temptation. He fathered a child out of wedlock, and at one point even asked God to grant him purity . . . "but not yet."[35] He wrote, "To love and to be loved was sweet to me, and all the more when I gained the enjoyment of the body of the person I loved. Thus I polluted the spring of friendship with the filth of concupiscence and I dimmed its luster with the slime of lust."[36]

Today, we know him as Saint Augustine. Later in life, he realized that as a youth he relied too heavily upon his own strength rather than God's. He wrote, "I thought that continence arose from one's own powers, which I did not recognize in myself. I was foolish enough not to know . . . that no one can be continent unless you grant it. For you would surely have granted it if my inner groaning had reached your ears and I with firm faith had cast my cares on you."[37]

Much like Augustine, we often fail at chastity because of an excessive sense of self-reliance. We are weak. But we can't use this as an excuse to sin. Devin Schadt explains, "A man may believe himself to be weak in the area of chastity, and rather than submitting his weakness to God and undergoing the process of redemption, he surrenders to Satan, believing that indulging in lust will grant him masculine strength. Man's strength, un-submitted to God, often subjects him to weakness, whereas man's weakness, submitted to God, makes him strong."[38]

Therefore, our greatest strength is the knowledge of our weakness. If pride goes before a fall, humility alone can sustain a chaste life. Perhaps this is why Jesus told the apostles, "Pray that you do not enter into temptation."[39] He knows how weak we are, and we ought to heed his advice. However, we don't often pray to avoid temptation, because we want to take some delight in it. Instead of avoiding temptation, we'd prefer to taste it, savor it for a moment, and then have the heroic willpower to overcome it. But Saint Josemaría Escrivá noted, "As soon as you willfully allow a dialogue with temptation to begin, the soul is robbed of peace, just as consent to impurity destroys grace."[40]

### Don't resent chastity.

When presented with the challenge of chastity, some men view it as nothing more than an obstacle to obtaining gratification. Karol Wojtyła explained:

> "The fact is that attaining or realizing a higher value demands a greater effort of will. So in order to spare ourselves the effort, to excuse our failure to obtain this value, we minimize its significance, deny it the respect which it deserves,

even see it as in some way evil, although objectivity requires us to recognize it as good. . . . Resentment . . . not only distorts the features of the good but devalues that which rightly deserves respect, so that man need not struggle to raise himself to the level of the true good, but can 'light-heartedly' recognize as good only what suits him, what is convenient and comfortable for him."[41]

Chastity does not require repression of sexual desire. It requires a healthy self-mastery over one's desires. This is why Dietrich Bonhoeffer wrote, "The essence of chastity is not the suppression of lust, but the total orientation of one's life towards a goal. Without such a goal, chastity is bound to become ridiculous. Chastity is the *sine qua non* of lucidity and concentration."[42]

Despite the popular misconception, sexual virtue does not lead to neurosis or misery. If anything, unchastity leads to these things. Archbishop Fulton Sheen remarked, "The sense of emptiness, melancholy, and frustration is a consequence of the failure to find infinite satisfaction in what is carnal and limited. Despair is disappointed hedonism. The most depressed spirits are those who seek God in a false god!"[43]

Therefore, if our goal is to love a woman rightly, there is no need to resent the message of chastity. Purity never destroys love. It defends it. Just as love makes chastity possible, chastity makes love possible. Like love, purity does not begin in the body, but in the will. We choose to love, and so we choose to be pure. To bring purity into a relationship is to bring Christ into the relationship, and where he is, there is peace and joy. This does present challenges, but as Saint John Paul II noted,

"Genuine love . . . is demanding. But its beauty lies precisely in the demands it makes."[44]

## Reset.

Many couples want to practice chastity but seem to fall repeatedly back into the same habits of going too far. They want to express God's love to each other, but often express affection without God's love. One couple I know continually went further than expected, and would often have the dreaded conversation: "I'm sorry. I didn't mean for things to go that far." "Me too, let's start over." After months living in this cycle of brief passion followed by prolonged regret and isolation, they realized that they were destroying their love. Despite their strong attractions and genuine feelings for each other, they knew that neither was spiritually mature enough to date. This was the core problem that wasn't being healed by their frequent talks about how they "don't want to do that again."

Therefore, they decided not to break up, but to take a bit of a "retreat" from the relationship, to get their spiritual lives in order. They took several months off the relationship—not to date anyone else, but to let God strengthen them in their ability to love. The man worked with a spiritual director to break free from pornography while the woman spent time in counseling to mend hurts from her past. It was a season to focus on God alone. During this time, it stung not to have the other constantly available, but this was just what they needed. They needed to sense what they could lose if they didn't salvage their love by getting their spiritual houses in order.

After several months off, they reunited and had a chaste courtship. It was a battle worth fighting, and they ended up saving their relationship, having a chaste engagement, and starting a family together.

## Find fellowship.

A man's strength can sometimes also be his greatest weakness, and this is certainly the case with self-reliance. Because of male pride, we often want to succeed on our own. But this is a recipe for failure when it comes to sexual purity. We need accountability and fellowship with other men who have the same standards.

If you play any sport with those who are less proficient than you are, you'll tend to overestimate your skill level, while making little improvement. On the other hand, if you compete against others who are more advanced, not only will you obtain a more realistic perspective of your own talent (or lack thereof), you'll also develop more efficiently as an athlete. The same is true in the moral life: If our friends are getting drunk every weekend, we think we deserve a halo for staying sober. If they're men of integrity, our faults become obvious.

One seventeenth-century spiritual writer compared true and false friendships with real honey and a poisonous form of it known as "Heraclean" honey.[45] When the dangerous honey is consumed, it is sweet to taste and causes an initial delight to the mind—much like the worldly friendships that offer superficial joys. However, the honey also confuses one's vision—much like false friendships blur one's judgment.

Living a virtuous life has never been easy. But there's no need to make it more difficult by choosing for our closest friends those who erode our resolutions to live a pure life. Therefore, it's not enough to have good friends. We need friends who are good. As Scripture explains, "Though a man might prevail against one who is alone, two will withstand him. A threefold cord is not quickly broken.[46] For this reason, when I speak to single women, I often tell them, "If you're interested in a man, take a close look at the men he chooses as his companions. This tells you almost everything you need to know about a man."

Throughout history, solid friendships have made men greater than they could ever have been without such fellowship. Take, for example, the Forty Martyrs of Sebaste. They were soldiers in the fourth century who served under Emperor Licinius but refused to burn incense to the pagan gods. In hopes of breaking their wills, the men were imprisoned and tortured. When all efforts failed, the men were handed over to be executed.

The governor Agricola marched them to a frozen lake and then ordered them to strip naked and stand on the icy waters throughout the night until they were dead. The Christian men encouraged each other, saying that one bad night would purchase them a happy eternity. On the shore of the lake, the pagan soldiers stood guard and lit a fire and a warm bath, inviting the men to apostatize, burn incense to the pagan gods, and live. As the night drew on, one can imagine the fog the soldiers' breath rising like incense to the true God, as they prayed, "Lord, we are forty engaged in this contest. Grant that forty may receive crowns and that we may not fall short of that sacred number."[47] One of the soldiers eventually succumbed to the pain and ran to the shore to abandon his faith, only to die as he reached the bath.

Meanwhile, one of the pagan soldiers who looked on was so impressed by the courage of the thirty-nine that he disrobed, declared himself a Christian, and joined them in giving his life.

Some survived longer than the torturers had expected, so their limbs were broken and their bodies were burned. The charred remains were cast into a river so that no memory of the men would remain.

However, seventeen centuries later, the pagan leaders and their gods have long since been forgotten, while icons of the Forty Martyrs of Sebaste can be found in churches throughout Eastern Christianity. In fact, within the Orthodox wedding ceremony is a prayer that mentions these men to the newlywed couple during their crowning, to remind them of the crown that awaits them in heaven if they persevere in the same way.

Imagine, though, if each of those men had been isolated, each assigned his own frozen pond. How many would have withstood the test? Because they were joined in prayer and brotherhood, they won the crown of martyrdom.

# PREPARE A PLACE FOR HER

Two thousand years ago, do you know what the first thing a Jewish man would do when proposing to his bride-to-be? He'd share a cup of wine with her, give her a few gifts as a pledge of his love . . . and then he'd leave her.

But he wasn't abandoning her. He was going to his father's house for twelve months to prepare a place for her. The father of the groom alone decided when the dwelling place was ready for her, and then, with his father's blessing, the young man would return to the bride, celebrate their marriage, and bring her into the bridal chamber of their new home to consummate their love.

For those familiar with the Gospels, the storyline is familiar. During the Last Supper, as Jesus shared the Passover wine with his apostles, he told them he would be leaving them. But he added: "Let not your hearts be troubled; believe in God, believe also in me. In my Father's house are many rooms; if it were not so, would I have told you that I go to prepare a place for you? And when I go and prepare a place for you, I will come again and will take you to myself, that where I am you may be also."[48]

In becoming man, Jesus not only revealed God to us, he revealed us to ourselves. He also revealed the proper order in which a man ought to court a woman. When he proposes to her, he enters a new dimension of their relationship, where he's tasked with the responsibility to prepare for their new life together. Once that is complete, and he has made a complete gift of himself to her, they become one.

What can today's man gain from this timeline? The world is preparing for marriage backward. The typical modern timeline now involves the two becoming sexually active, the couple cohabiting, and then the marriage ceremony follows. Once the honeymoon ends, the couple returns to the life they've already known for several years. What if men chose to upturn this model and courted women as Christ courted his bride? Consider what that would look like.

## Suffering Servant

Following a wedding ceremony, the norm during most wedding receptions is for the bride to take a seat while encircled by her wedding guests. The groom approaches her, reaches up her dress, and pulls her garter off. He then tosses this undergarment to a frothing mob of single men who grapple to catch it as an omen of good luck.

However, an increasing number of Christian grooms are discontinuing this tradition and integrating a new ritual into their wedding reception. As usual, the bride takes a seat in the presence of all their friends and family. But, instead of venturing under her dress to the roars of the crowd, he approaches her with a pitcher of water, a bowl, and a towel. He then takes a knee, removes her shoes, and washes her feet, as Christ washed the feet of his bride, the Church, on the night before he gave his life for her.

These grooms are not putting on a show for their wedding guests. They sincerely believe their brides deserve to be loved in such a manner. They know that Christ initiated his gift of love to his bride by becoming a suffering servant. He used his strength not to dominate, but to serve.

In order to have a joyful marriage and family, each member of the family must learn to serve the others. The husband is called to model Christ's headship in this regard. Therefore, one of the best preparations for family life is for a man to give himself in service. A man's character expands when he learns to live for others. A good way to do this is for the man to get involved in what he feels passionate about: Volunteer for youth groups, serve the homeless, give a year or two as a missionary, serve at an orphanage, join pro-life apostolates, and so on. And not that you should do it for this reason, but countless spouses have found one another by doing just this.

As good as it is for a man to serve strangers, the most essential and immediate context in which a man learns authentic love is within his own family. If he is unable to exercise patience and loving service with the people who live under his roof today, his marriage will be no different.

This is *the* greatest form of marriage preparation, because if a man can love the people he lives with, he can love anyone. "Love thy neighbor" requires minimal effort because those individuals live down the street and you hardly see them. However, loving and forgiving the people you share a home with is demanding. Therefore, real marriage preparation isn't about spending three hours a day texting one another. It's about learning to love, to be patient, to forgive, and to say, "I'm sorry" (repeatedly).

As one man noted:

"[F]ulfillment does not lie in comfort, ease, and following one's inclinations, but precisely in allowing demands to be made upon you, in taking the harder path. Everything else turns out somehow boring, anyway. Only the man who 'risks the fire,' who recognizes a calling within himself, a vocation, an ideal he must satisfy, who takes on real responsibility, will find fulfillment. As we have said, it is not in taking, not on the path of comfort, that we become rich, but only in giving."[49]

## Unconditional Love

When a man thinks of preparing a place for his bride, his first inclination may be to think of the financial preparations needed to build a home. Or, he may consider the preparations needed to welcome her into his current living space. They might need to share a closet and her appropriation of their bathroom space might be something of a hostile takeover. In other words, he'll need to be flexible in creating space for her within their shared domestic life.

While these are good aspirations, there is a more fundamental preparation that the woman requires. She needs for him to prepare in his heart a place for her. He might feel that he's already done that by choosing to marry her, but in many cases the woman brings into a marriage experiences from her past that the man has trouble accepting. He may welcome her into his life, while holding over her head the decisions that she may have made in the past with other men.

My wife was raised in a fatherless home, and often shares her story with young women about how she was sexually abused as a child, lost her virginity at the age of fifteen, and lived a lifestyle that left her wounded and ashamed. She experienced a beautiful conversion and embraced the virtue of chastity for several years before the two of us met. Meanwhile, I had saved my virginity for marriage. Because of our situation, countless men have reached out to me because they're trying to reconcile the love they feel for their girlfriends, fiancées, or wives with the angst they feel about their past.

Some express to me the pit they feel in their stomachs when they think about their partner being so intimate with another man. They wrestle with feelings of resentment, jealousy, insecurity, and disappointment. If not healed, these negative emotions will fester within the relationship and potentially destroy it.

One reason why such thoughts continue to plague certain men is that they're probably trying to push the thoughts out of their mind without dealing with them. Sweeping them under the rug will allow them to continue bothering them. Therefore, the solution is not to repress these thoughts but to deal with them by accepting them and lifting them up. If you find yourself in this situation, here are five steps to work through it together:

### Thank God.

Act against feelings of bitterness and hurt by thanking God for bringing her out of that lifestyle. This will help to keep resentment from infecting your relationship. Remember: She wasn't unfaithful to you. She just made some poor choices, and most likely regrets them. If you're like me, you've made some mistakes in your past, too, whether it be looking at pornography, or acting impurely with other women. Remember that resentment is a choice, not just an emotion. You need to actively reject and uproot it.

### Offer it up.

Instead of dwelling on her past and moping over it, lift those thoughts to God when they come to mind. Here's how: When you begin to think of her previous actions and relationships, take that as a reminder to pray for the healing of her memories and for the conversion of the men she dated. Because of Christ's sufferings, our trials in life have redemptive value when we accept them with faith and offer them up to him. You need to realize the good that the Lord can do through it. Use your suffering to bring grace to others. In other words, let the pain become a prayer.

### Live pure.

Resolve to lead a pure life with her. You might not be the one to marry her one day, and if that is the case, you don't want to add more regrets for her to bring into her future marriage. In order to live a pure life, you also need to make sure that you're not looking at pornography. This will infect the wound in your relationship and intensify your insecurities because it will make the thoughts of her past become more visual in your imagination.

### Talk to her.

If the relationship is heading toward marriage, do not be afraid to talk to her about the struggle you are experiencing. It is better that these issues come to the surface before marriage than within it. If you do not feel ready for this, perhaps you can speak with a pastor, parent, or some other counselor you respect (without betraying her privacy and trust). In other words, it's best to talk to someone who either already knows her past, or who does not know her at all.

Remember that good relationships require open and honest communication. When you bring up your concerns, make sure not to blame her for the past, but rather express the fact that you want to work through this issue together. Never hold this over her or use it against her. Instead, share your insecurities, fears, or hurts, and allow her to love you. This will require some vulnerability on your part and some patience and empathy from her. If your love is strong and forgiving, the two of you will be able to overcome this difficulty.

When you do this, do not get very specific with regard to things she did with the guy(s). Such information will do more harm than good. Previous intimacies of one partner often cause feelings of pain, inferiority, or resentment in the other. Talking through your struggle will help you to guard your heart from the poison of unforgiveness. But take it easy on her, and don't drag it on forever, which will cause her to resent you. I had once heard that a young man approached Saint Padre Pio in tears because his girlfriend broke up with him. The pastor smacked him in the face and said, "Be a man." As harsh as that sounds, it's just what the guy needed.

It is entirely reasonable for you to feel hurt by her past. This is natural. It's not a sign that you haven't forgiven her. It's just a sign that you have a human heart. Forgiving someone is not about numbness. It's about no longer holding something against that person. It's a decision, not a feeling. In time, the wounds will heal, but it's not within your power not to feel a certain way. Hopefully she'll be patient with you as you work through this. As a note of encouragement, I have found that over time it gets better, and that in our case, marriage has been healing. For example, even though the woman you're with may have experienced sexual activity in the past, marital intimacy will be unique for her, because she has never experienced the gift of sexual intimacy as God intended—as a sacrament.

If you find that the issue is not improving, but is driving a wedge of resentment between you, find a marital counselor to talk with. Marriage is one of the most important decisions you will ever make, and you need to surround yourself with wise counselors. The woman you are with should not have to live with the cloud of her past forever hovering above her. Your task is to help cast it away.

### Reflect the love of God to her.

A man in this situation once emailed me, saying how he felt somewhat "gypped" because of his fiancée's past. I can understand why he would feel that. However, men should not save themselves for the sake of getting, but for giving. So much of authentic love is simply about giving and not seeking something in return. On the day of your wedding, you might not receive the gift of your wife's virginity. But you will receive something greater: the gift of herself. It would be sad to lose the gift of a person in pursuit of the gift of virginity. In fact, I know of one such couple who was nearing engagement but ended up breaking off the relationship because the man could not accept the woman's past. It was tragic, because he could not see that in failing to accept her past, he was forfeiting a beautiful future. But if a man is so obsessed with defining a woman by her past that he can't see who she has become today, then he doesn't deserve to be a part of her future.

Consider how unconditionally God loves us, and how stingy we are in return. In fact, the Bible often speaks about Israel as having played the harlot, and having forgotten her first love, which was God. Yet God forgave her iniquities and loved Israel despite the past. I'm not comparing your partner to a harlot (or you to God) but am simply saying that you'll be loving her in a godly way if you choose to accept her past. She'll need to love you unconditionally as well, if you hope to have a lasting marriage. We all have our own imperfections. God does not hold a grudge over her, and neither should you.

Your unconditional acceptance of your potential future bride makes you more of a man in her eyes than anything else you can do. She may wonder, "Am I worthy of love? Am I damaged goods? Am I unlovable?" You play an important role in her healing, through dying to yourself for love of her. Believe it or not, this wound you feel is actually given to you by God in order to heal your own soul. It will conform you to Christ, purify your love, and even strengthen your marriage if you continue to respond to God's grace to carry this cross. Both of you play a role in each other's healing, and you can't lose sight of that.

In summary, the main thing you need to do is to have a grateful heart for the woman she has become and be patient with yourself and with her when these emotions rise up within you. Use them as a reminder to pray for her healing, resolve to keep your relationship pure, and show her the love of God. When unpleasant thoughts of her past arise, turn inward in prayer, and say, "God, I choose this because you allow it. I accept it for love of you. May you be glorified through this." Do these things, and in His time, God will heal the wounds in her and even in you. In the meantime, do not fear that these haunting thoughts of the past will never diminish. Over the course of time, you should feel greater peace as your love deepens.

## Wait for the Father's Blessing

On our wedding day, as I stood before the altar, I saw Crystalina's silhouette through the stained-glass windows in the back door of the church. The doors swung open, the violin and organ music played, and she began walking toward me, gazing at me through her veil. As this was happening, I had an overwhelming thought of God the Father's hands behind her, giving her to me as a gift.

Since she did not have a father in her life, a man who loved her as a foster-father walked her down the aisle to me. He was a burly man, having played rugby in England, weighing well over 250 pounds, and standing at least a foot taller than her. When they approached the altar, he lifted her veil, leaned town to kiss her cheek, and gave her to me with a firm handshake and a proud smile. I felt something take place at that moment. Until that moment, he was her man. But with the giving of the bride, that gift and responsibility had been transferred to me.

As a man prepares for marriage, he awaits the gift of his bride not only from her father, but from God the Father. This is not a ritualistic formality. It is a reality. By reserving for marriage the forms of affection that belong rightly only within marriage, a man is honoring her earthly father and her heavenly Father.

Following a couple's engagement, it's natural for them to feel as if they're almost married. But this feeling often grows into a tempting sense of entitlement for them gradually to become more physically intimate as the wedding day approaches. Even devout Christian couples who are trying their best to wait for the wedding night might think, "We've already bought the rings and put a down payment on the house. It's not like we just met. It's okay for us to go further than before."

When this mentality begins to creep in, it helps to remember that ten minutes before a man and woman marry, they are just as married as they were the day before they met. Although an engaged couple might feel 99 percent married, marriage is a bit like pregnancy, in that a person either is or is not. It's all or nothing. In the same way, the forms of affection that are proper to express within marriage (including deliberate sexual arousal) do not become gradually permissible as the wedding becomes closer. Instead, a couple should take even greater measures to guard one another's soul as they prepare to receive this sacrament and the gift of one another.

This will undoubtedly require sacrifice. But a man who truly loves will not run from the cross. In the words of Devin Schadt, the deepest ontological truth of man is that "man is essentially programmed to sacrifice himself on behalf of his bride to ensure that she be sanctified."[50] This isn't something we are obligated to do. It's who we're created to be. A man who loves in such a manner knows that no pleasure on earth could be more desirable than his longing to be with a woman for eternity.

To develop and guard this love, remember that from a Christian perspective, the wedding bed is not a mattress. It's an altar. It's where a sacrament is consummated. The author of Hebrews states that the marriage bed must not be defiled (Heb. 13:4). But you can't defile something that isn't sacred, and for something to be sacred, it means that it is set apart. The bed itself is holy. It's where a covenant is sealed. Therefore, unmarried couples have no place upon it. It is reserved for a godly purpose, and that purpose is for the bride and groom to express their wedding vows in and through their bodies. By doing so, they make visible the invisible love of God.

In his poem, "Pre-Sacrament," Karol Wojtyła explains:

And when they became "one flesh"
—that wondrous union—
on the horizon there appears the mystery of fatherhood and
    motherhood.
—They returned to the source of life within them.
—They returned to the Beginning.
—Adam knew his wife
and she conceived and gave birth.
They know that they have crossed the threshold of the great-
    est responsibility!

# 6

## CLEAVE TO HER

Immediately following the creation of the woman, the book of Genesis declares, "Therefore a man leaves his father and his mother and cleaves to his wife, and they become one flesh" (Gen. 2:24). The ancient Hebrew word for "cleave" in this passage is *dâbaq*. While it is often translated as to cleave, to cling, or to join together, the word also means *to pursue closely*. Consider the potential deeper meaning here: a man leaves his parents and doesn't simply cling to his wife . . . he pursues her *after* he marries her.

What this means is that the tips offered earlier in this book on how to pursue a woman are not meant to be used merely in the courtship phase of a relationship to win a woman's heart. They need to be implemented until death do you part. This is the main reason so many people today don't know how to date: Their parents forgot how to do it! If the family is the school of love, countless young people have been sitting in a classroom without an instructor.

The best way for a young man to learn how to date is for him to be blessed with a father who truly cleaves to his wife. For example, a friend of mine has been married for nearly twenty years and has never missed his weekly date night with his bride! Rain or shine, they make the effort to get away from the children and the chaotic demands of domestic life in order to reconnect and rekindle their love. To them, the wedding was not a finish line within their relationship. If anything, it was more of a beginning. Consider what one priest stated at another friend's wedding: "Today should be the day you love each other the least. Every year, your love should grow more than the year before." While this sounds ideal and romantic, is it possible?

It is. But in order for it to happen, patience is required by the couple to allow their love to mature. The qualities that may have initially drawn them to one another may evolve over time. For example, Archbishop Fulton Sheen wrote:

"Beauty in a woman and strength in a man are two of the most evident spurs to love. Physical beauty and vitality increase vigor in each other, but it is to be noticed that beauty in a woman and strength in a man are given by God to serve purposes of allurement. They come at that age of life when men and women are urged to marry one another. They are not permanent possessions. They are something like frosting on a cake, or like the electric starter of an automobile motor. If love were based only on the fact that she is a model and he is a fullback on the football team, marriage would never endure. But just as frosting on the cake leads to the cake itself, so too do these allurements pass on to greater treasures. Once on congratulating a wife who had a very handsome husband we heard her reply: 'I no longer notice that he is handsome; I notice now that he has greater qualities.'"[51]

This couple knew from experience that a healthy marriage is not measured by the quantity of years, but by the quality of love.

Is there a secret ingredient to building such love? I once heard of two pastors who had a lengthy discussion about why some married couples in their churches had thriving marriages while others did not. They noticed how some couples seemed to enter marriage with the odds stacked against them and enjoyed lasting love, while others who seemed to have it all together had marriages that imploded and ended in divorce. The two pastors stayed up late into the night discussing the matter and came to one conclusion as to what makes a marriage last: The couples who last are the ones who show up and fight for their marriages when things get tough. That's it.

## Breaking Idols

Based upon one's families of origin, couples enter into marriage with an unspoken set of healthy and unhealthy expectations of what spousal life is going to look like. While some people approach marriage with an idealized image of it, others have created an idolized image of it. Such a person might read theology books and see filtered social media photos of seemingly perfect marriages and families and expect his future to look no different. Although the ideal of marriage needs to be defended, the idol of marriage needs to be broken. Otherwise, as C.S. Lewis remarked, all idols will eventually break the hearts of their worshippers.[52]

If one makes an idol out of his expectations of marriage, assuming it will be an endless honeymoon, the following happens: Within marriage, the demands of true love begin to weigh down upon couples. As this occurs, their shortcomings rise to the surface in equal measure. This takes place in every marriage. Whereas couples may have assumed prior to marriage that they excelled in virtues such as patience, forgiveness, and sacrificial love, it may very well be that those qualities had never seriously been put to the test before.

When the faults of both spouses surface, many couples assume they made the wrong choice of a marriage partner. While this is sometimes the case (even Jesus mentioned that some marriages are invalid),[53] more often than not, the sacrament is doing its job. It is bringing the faults of the spouses to the surface like oil in water, so that those imperfections might be healed. Prior to marriage, those imperfections were still present, but were lying dormant under the surface of a more comfortable life. Within marriage, one's faults are no longer hidden—they're under a magnifying glass.

Therefore, marriage often involves a painful process of purification. It may feel to the spouses as if God had placed them in a winepress. Such suffering may cause one or both spouses to question God, wondering if he duped them into choosing this life. During such times, it helps to recall the process by which diamonds are created. Buried within the earth's crust for countless years, these gems are forged under the weight of unfathomable pressure. In the same way, the sufferings of married life are often unseen, prolonged, and intense. But if one allows the design process to reach its completion, the result is something glorious.

## The Cross

Each spouse is likely to be tested and tempted in their own way to retreat from the process of purification. I once read that a woman's loyalty is tested when her man has nothing, but a man's loyalty is tested when he has everything. No matter what form the test takes, the husband is presented with a choice. Does he remain upon the cross or does he descend from it?

Archbishop Sheen declared:

> "This world of ours is full of half-completed Gothic cathedrals, of half-finished lives and half-crucified souls. Some carry the Cross to Calvary and then abandon it; others are nailed to it and detach themselves before the elevation; others are crucified, but in answer to the challenge of the world 'Come down,' they come down after one hour . . . two hours . . . after two hours and fifty-nine minutes. Real Christians are they who persevere unto the end. Our Lord stayed until He had finished."[54]

In response to the weight of the cross, some men flee marriage altogether. Others retreat into false consolations such as emotional or physical affairs, busyness, emotional coldness, pornography, or fantasies of an easier life. For every spouse, temptations will seem their strongest when consolations are weakest. For example, when a husband feels dismissed, disrespected, or disappointed by his wife, other women will exude a greater allure. However, as the saying goes, "If the grass is always greener on the other side, maybe it's time to water your own grass." Moments of desolation in marriage are not indications that a man ought to flee his post. In fact, if a husband puts down his cross, he always lays it upon on the shoulders of his wife and children.

While undergoing trials within marriage, husbands may be tempted to believe that they are unique or special in their suffering. They assume that their situation must be worse than the lot given to other men, and they may even begin to pity themselves. They begin to harbor feelings of entitlement, resentment, and unhealthy curiosity. No one spoke more eloquently of this situation than the author of *The Lord of the Rings*, J.R.R. Tolkien, when he wrote about the secret to a happy marriage:

"Men are not [monogamous]. No good pretending. Men just ain't, not by their animal nature. Monogamy (although it has long been fundamental to our inherited ideas) is for us men a piece of 'revealed' ethic, according to faith and not the flesh. The essence of a fallen world is that the best cannot be attained by free enjoyment, or by what is called 'self-realization' (usually a nice name for self-indulgence, wholly inimical to the realization of other selves); but by denial, by suffering. Faithfulness in Christian marriages entails that: great mortification.

For a Christian man there is no escape. Marriage may help to sanctify and direct to its proper object his sexual desires; its grace may help him in the struggle; but the struggle remains. It will not satisfy him—as hunger may be kept off by regular meals. It will offer as many difficulties to the purity proper to that state as it provides easements.

No man, however truly he loved his betrothed and bride as a young man, has lived faithful to her as a wife in mind and body without deliberate conscious exercise of the will, without self-denial. Too few are told that—even those brought up in 'the Church.' Those outside seem seldom to have heard it.

When the glamour wears off, or merely works a bit thin, they think that they have made a mistake, and that the real soul-mate is still to find. The real soul-mate too often proves to be the next sexually attractive person that comes along.

Someone whom they might indeed very profitably have married, if only—. Hence divorce, to provide the 'if only.'

And of course they are as a rule quite right: they did make a mistake. Only a very wise man at the end of his life could make a sound judgement concerning whom, amongst the total possible chances, he ought most profitably have married! Nearly all marriages, even happy ones, are mistakes: in the sense that almost certainly (in a more perfect world, or even with a little more care in this very imperfect one) both partners might have found more suitable mates. But the 'real soul-mate' is the one you are actually married to. In this fallen world, we have as our only guides, prudence, wisdom (rare in youth, too late in age), a clean heart, and fidelity of will . . ."[55]

Therefore, at the moments when a man is tempted to pity himself and withdraw from his mission, God calls him to remain upon the cross. Jesus, in fact, never descended from the cross himself. He remained upon it until he was taken down. In the same way, God has placed the husband at the head of his family to be an image of Christ the priest, prophet, and king. Christ the king brings order to his kingdom by modeling true servanthood. Christ the prophet sanctifies his people through his example more than through his words. Christ the priest teaches his family the meaning of sacrifice by becoming the sacrificial offering himself.

## God Heals Through Affliction

When you encounter suffering within your vocation, remember that God isn't asking you to enjoy the cross, but to embrace it. As Saint Peter Claver once said, "Love does not mean that I like to do what I'm doing, love means that I do it."[56] This was said by a man who would enter into the festering and disease-infested hulls of ships to minister to the thousands of slaves who entered the port of Cartagena daily in the seventeenth century. Lest we begin to feel sorry for ourselves, it helps to remember that countless men like him have carried weightier crosses than our own.

Consider the story of the martyrdom of the seven brothers, found in the ancient Jewish text of 2 Maccabees. In it, seven brothers and their mother refused to transgress the laws of God in order to appease a wicked king. In response to their defiance:

> "The king fell into a rage, and gave orders that pans and caldrons be heated. These were heated immediately, and he commanded that the tongue of their spokesman be cut out and that they scalp him and cut off his hands and feet, while the rest of the brothers and the mother looked on. When he was utterly helpless, the king ordered them to take him to the fire, still breathing, and to fry him in a pan. The smoke from the pan spread widely, but the brothers and their mother encouraged one another to die nobly, saying, 'The Lord God is watching over us and in truth has compassion on us.'"[57]

One by one, the seven brothers were tortured because they refused to violate the law of God. But consider their remarkable faith! In the midst of their agony, they declared, "The Lord God is watching over us and in truth has compassion on us." Compassion? The man is being cooked in a frying pan! Similarly, the author of Hebrews wrote, "whom the Lord loves, he disciplines; he scourges every son he acknowledges."[58] How can we reconcile such language with a loving and tender Father?

Saint Augustine answered, "Understanding is the reward given by faith. Do not try to understand in order to believe, but believe in order to understand."[59] In other words, if God is a loving Father, then he must have a plan to bring some greater good from the trials he allows his children to experience. Human understanding is not a prerequisite for God's providence to work. What's needed is trust. For as much as we look for God to balance the scales of suffering in this life, we need to remember that he has all eternity to do this. As one Christian remarked, "It is because of faith that we exchange the present for the future."[60]

But what good could come from suffering in this life? The book of Job answers, "He delivers the afflicted by their affliction, and opens their ear by adversity."[61] Like a good surgeon, the wounds that God inflicts are sometimes necessary to bring healing. As noted in the book of Job, one of the fruits of adversity is that one's ears become open to God. A man's affliction brings about his deliverance. How so?

I know of a man who entered marriage with every good intention and hope to build a happy and holy family. However, several years into marriage he began to feel chafed, discouraged, and exhausted. He felt like he had never done a push-up before but was now being asked to compete in the CrossFit Games. He began to look fondly back upon the freedoms and pleasures he enjoyed prior to his current relationship. His affection for these things lingered strongly within him, and marriage began to feel like a prison.

His former way of life afforded him effortless pleasure without much responsibility. But God wanted to draw him into a deeper level of maturity in his love. After he abandoned his bachelorhood in exchange for the permanent and faithful bond of marriage, it felt restricting until he realized that this new "prison" was his only hope of being truly free.

In time, he saw what God was doing in his heart. In the past, he had only expressed romantic attention to a woman for the sake of getting something from her. Tenderness was a means to an end. Within marriage, he was learning how to be affectionate, thoughtful, and romantic for the sake of his wife, without expecting anything in return.

As he was considering whether marriage was worth the effort, I emailed him:

"Think back to the days when you first fell in love with her. Remember how you dreamed of giving her everything. Reawaken that desire. Pursue your wife as if she was a single woman who you wanted to impress and date. God is giving you this task, so embrace it with all of your heart, seeking all the graces you'll need from God. Let him love your bride through you. It's his love she needs the most, and God has chosen you to become the means through which this healing love can be poured out onto your family. Make no mistake: This is the fight of your life. God is meeting you in the struggle, and he wants to sanctify both you and your family in the process. In the meantime, guard your heart from the idea of being loved by another woman better than your wife loves you. Let go of it. One of the scars of pornography is the vice of thinking there's always someone better. Don't pamper yourself with fantasies and the dream of such affections. Kill them, for love of your wife and daughters. Don't just refuse the sin—refuse to hold any affection for the idea of it. If you guard your heart, you will begin to guard your eyes. You must win the hidden battles before you can become victorious over the visible ones."

Through a long and challenging season of marriage, this husband came to learn that chastity is not something that a man needs to practice *until* marriage. Rather, the virtue of chastity sustains marriage itself. Whereas abstinence is merely the absence of sex, chastity is the presence of a pure mind, heart, and body. It requires self-mastery and purity of intention. Without these abilities, a man will see his wife as an outlet for his sexual needs, rather than his beloved companion.

## A Man's Rights

When chastity is practiced prior to marriage, it prepares one for the requirements of chastity within marriage. This may be a confusing notion because the word "chastity" is often confused with "abstinence." While abstinence is the absence of sex, chastity is the proper use of the gift of sexuality, depending upon one's state in life. So, for a single person, chastity does involve abstinence. For a married man, it involves fidelity, purity of heart, reverence for God's plan for sexuality, and even abstinence at times.

When chastity is practiced before marriage, not only does it train a man in faithfulness, it also teaches him that abstinence itself can be an expression of love. However, when the virtue is not developed before marriage, chaste married love can feel like an excessive burden.

Like it or not, abstinence is a part of marriage. Sometimes, it must be practiced to a heroic degree. Take, for example, another friend of mine. When his wife was a young girl, she was sexually abused. Ten years into their marriage, her memories began to resurface. Flashbacks began to haunt her, and she told him she could not be sexually intimate with him while she was trying to process all her emotions and memories. Being the understanding man that he is, he assured her that they could work through this together as she began going to counseling. A week of abstinence went by. And then a month. And then six months.

At this point, the husband was wrestling with God over the situation, thinking, "God, don't I have needs and rights?" God spoke to his heart, telling him: "Yes, you have rights. You have a right to have it all be about you. You have a right to have your needs met. You have a right not to be heroic. You have every right to not become a saint."

The husband responded to this challenge and loved his bride patiently, expressing love to her in nonsexual ways. During this season of abstinence, he discovered that this was an opportunity for his own purification and healing. Culture teaches men that their masculinity is measured by a woman's sexual responsiveness to them. When a woman is frigid, distant, and unavailable, it may cause them to feel like less of a man. But by remaining on this cross for love of his bride, this man was becoming more of a man to her than any she had ever known before. The two worked through this issue as a team and were blessed with a strengthened marriage.

Imagine if this man did not understand how abstinence could be an expression of love. Imagine if he grew petulant, cold, and distant toward his wife as the months added up, because she wasn't meeting his "needs." His wounded masculinity would only have infected and deepened her emotional wounds. But through this affliction, both were healed in their own way.

When the demands of chaste love within marriage arise, the temptation may be to blame chastity, marriage, or even monogamy as the problem. But these things are not the cause of the problem. They're merely the God-given means by which our deepest imperfections of self-absorption, lust, and immaturity flare up. God allows them to surface so that they can be uprooted and healed. We're given the chance to ask ourselves, "How much of the strain is from marriage, and how much of the strain is because I entered marriage as a deeply selfish person? Is our relationship the problem, or is the real problem that I have a propensity to do all things so that I might benefit from them in one way or another?" Obviously, it takes a great deal of humility to answer these questions honestly. But the degree to which we can be honest with ourselves is the extent to which God can heal us.

During such trials, it is best to keep in mind the words of Saint Paul, who wrote, "No temptation has overtaken you that is not common to man. God is faithful, and he will not let you be tempted beyond your strength, but with the temptation will also provide the way of escape, that you may be able to endure it."[62] In effect, he's saying to husbands, "Do you really think you're unique in the temptations that you're feeling, as if every married man hasn't felt them? Do you think that all the husbands who persevered until the end in pure fidelity to their brides and children were somehow immune from the same challenges, and you're the one guy who has all the unmet desires and disappointments?" Don't take the easy route and blame marriage and monogamy. The brokenness is within us.

Lest one feel discouraged by such an honest reproach, Saint Paul encourages us that God offers us a way to escape and endure the trial. He promises that "I am sure that he who began a good work in you will bring it to completion."[63] The key here is remembering who began the good work, and who will complete it: God.

Such trials are not merely allowed by God's permissive will. Padre Pio declared, "Suffering is a gift from God; blessed is he who knows how to profit by it."[64] When suffering comes, it's not often in the form that men prefer. Whereas women often have a great capacity to suffer internally for the sake of love, men prefer to externalize their devotion. We want to kill dragons and storm castles. However, Dr. Alice von Hildebrand points out that a man's innate desire for heroism must find its place in the

"modest deeds of everyday life, and will transform the tiresome routine of daily duties into golden threads binding oneself closer and closer to the beloved. There is in conjugal love a note of truth which is lacking in romantic love. It is a love that has been tested in the furnace of everyday trials and difficulties and has come out victoriously. . . . To be kind and lovable for a moment is no great feat. But to be loving day after day in the most varied and trying circumstances can be achieved only by a man who truly loves."[65]

## Lead in Love

For one of our wedding anniversaries, I crafted a wooden kneeler for two as a gift to my wife, so that we could kneel beside each other when we prayed. During a particularly difficult season of marriage, I walked into our room after an argument with her, and knelt there alone, looking up at the crucifix. She and I had reached an impasse and could not see eye to eye on some topic that I can't even remember. No one was budging, and so I asked God, "Who is right? Am I right, or is she right? If she's right, show me. I'm pretty sure I'm right, though." I'm not one who often hears the voice of God clearly, but on that day, I did. All he said was, "It doesn't matter who is right. Just love her." Honestly, this was a disappointing answer, because I was rather curious as to whether or not I was right. But I knew it was just what I needed to hear.

As a friend of mine once told me, "In marriage, you can either be right or you can be happy. But you can't be both." For those who have temperaments that are stubborn, this can create quite an interesting dynamic. Every man has his share of pride and egoism, and there's perhaps no greater remedy available for man than the sacrament of marriage. One spiritual writer even remarked, "The state of marriage is one which requires more virtue and constancy than any other; it is a perpetual exercise of mortification."[66] Don't fear the challenge, though, because as Joseph Barth remarked, "Marriage is our last, best chance to grow up."

Because the challenges of marriage can be so great, a man must know where his strength comes from. In short, a man will love as he prays. One prayerful husband I know told me that a man's love for his wife and family can be measured by the degree to which he protects his interior life. Ponder the depth of his words: the degree to which a man guards his prayer life and his soul is the measure of a man's love for his wife and children.

How can a man's love be gauged in this way? God is love, and a man cannot give what he has not received. The man who wishes to grow in love must carve out time every day for his relationship with God. He must make room in his life for contemplation if he hopes to transmit the love of God to others. Ultimately, manhood in its purest form is not something that a male *achieves*. Manhood is *received* when men accept the love of God the Father.

Some may think, "Well, I'm not really spiritual." But this is as accurate as thinking, "I'm not really physical." We're both, and a man is only half alive if he disregards his spiritual life. While speaking to college students, Karol Wojtyła remarked, "The lack of prayer can never be taken to mean that you do not need prayer. Indeed, the longer we do not pray, the greater the need grows, so that at a certain moment it explodes in the search for some outlet."[67]

In the spiritual life, no one stands still. One is either moving forward or backward. If you feel that you're not progressing toward God because your spiritual life seems dry, remember that one is saved by God, not by one's feelings of his nearness. At times, aridity in prayer is caused by our slothful and tepid attitude toward it. Other times, God weans sensible consolations away from man in prayer, in order to purify his faith. Whatever the case may be, where should you begin?

Here's a simple game plan: Do whatever God tells you. How do you know what he wishes to say? Listen to him. How do you learn to listen? Give him the chance to speak to your heart in silence. How do you do that? Make time for prayer. If we guard our interior lives of prayer, we tap into the deep source of infinite love. If we pull away from this, the well of our human capacity to love will run dry.

## The Ultimate Love Story

You may wonder why I dedicated so much of this final chapter to the difficulties and sufferings of married life. It may seem like a rather bleak and foreboding ending to what began as an otherwise pleasant dating manual. One reason is that you'll need no advice on how to savor the joys of marriage. Those times will take care of themselves. However, in one way or another, Christ crucified will visit many men within their marriages. When this happens, he asks us not to be afraid.

Although marriage may seem far away, Christ also wishes to accompany you in all the years that precede your marriage. If you reflect upon all the dating advice in this book, you'll notice that all of it is an allegory of the love of Jesus Christ for his bride, the Church. He initiated the relationship, pursued her with sincerity, and committed to her with clarity. He left his Father in heaven and his mother on earth in order to give his body to his bride on the Cross, so that she might have his life within her. Now, he has gone to prepare a place for her, so that where he is, she will be with him forever.

God is love, and when a man loves a woman rightly, he performs the greatest work of evangelization possible: making the invisible love of God visible to the world. This is your task. Go do it.

# DISCUSSION QUESTIONS

## Chapter One: Love Your Bride Before You Meet Her

What strategies in your own life have you found to be helpful in battling temptations?

Have you noticed that temptation seems strongest when you're bored, lonely, angry, stressed, or tired? Is one of these a stronger trigger than the others?

Which of the three points from Saint Ignatius of Loyola's Spiritual Exercises did you find most useful?

Do you feel that thinking about what kind of man you want to be for your future spouse or family would help you resist the allure of pornography? Or does it seem too far removed?

## Chapter Two: Is She the One?

Can you think of two points you could add to the section on knowing if she's the right woman to date?

Can you think of two points you might add to the section on knowing if it's the right time to date?

What are five essential qualities you would hope to find in a future wife?

Should there be any differences in what a man is looking for in a girlfriend versus what he hopes to find in a wife? Why?

## Chapter Three: Ask Her Out!

Which dating tip did you find most surprising, and which was most helpful?

What do you think about Jason's assertion: "Asking a woman out is a win-win situation. Either you end up with a date, or you end up with clarity. Either way, it's better than being alone and unsure."

If college students reported that they'd rather have a traditional romantic relationship than a hookup, why do you think so many people settle for less?

What do you think keeps men from asking women on dates?

## Chapter Four: Date Your Soulmate

Have you noticed in your own life or the lives of your friends how couples sometimes date without knowing when their dating relationship began?

Which of the ten strategies on guarding your love did you find most helpful?

Have you ever prayed that you might not enter into temptation?

Where can men in your community go in order to find godly

friendships? Is this community doing enough to reach out to other men to make their presence known?

## Chapter Five: Prepare a Place for Her

Would you consider washing your bride's feet at your own wedding reception one day, rather than tossing her garter?

It was stated that the greatest form of marriage preparation is loving the people you live with today, especially one's family. Do you agree?

What do you think of Devin Schadt's quote that the deepest ontological truth of man is that "man is essentially programmed to sacrifice himself on behalf of his bride to ensure that she be sanctified"?

Have you ever heard the idea that a wedding bed is an altar, and not simply a mattress? What did you think of this?

## Chapter Six: Cleave to Her

In what ways do you think men sometimes make an idol out of marriage?

The two pastors mentioned in the chapter said that the married couples who last are the ones who show up and fight for their marriages when things get tough. When things get tough, what are three things a couple can do to show up and fight for their love?

Have you ever considered abstinence to be an expression of love, either before or during marriage?

What is your reaction to J.R.R. Tolkien's excerpt on the secret to a happy marriage?

What did you think of the concluding point, that when we pursue women the way Jesus loved his bride, we make the love of God visible?

# ENDNOTES

1   Into the Breach: An Apostolic Exhortation from Bishop Thomas J. Olmsted to the Men of the Diocese of Phoenix, quoting Dr. Paul Vitz, Lecture, February 21, 2015.

2   Song 2:15.

3   Joseph Cardinal Ratzinger, *God and the World* (San Francisco: Ignatius, 2002), 421.

4   *Midrash Rabbah* on Genesis 22:6, in *The Soncino Midrash Rabbah* (New York: Judaica Press, 1983).

5   *The Collected Letters of C.S. Lewis, Vol. 3.* (New York: HarperCollins, 2007), 758–59.

6   Michael Moynihan, *The Father and His Family* (New York: Scepter, 2017), 72.

7   Matt. 5:29–30.

8   Jeffrey Satinover, M.D., *Feathers of the Skylark* (Westport, Conn.: Hamewith Books, 1996), 80–81.

9   Saint Basil of Caesarea, *De Spiritu Sancto*; Cf. Bryans Burroughs, "The Sign of the Cross," Catholic Answers (July 1, 1990).

10  Associated Press, "Anderson Gives Speech on Past Sexual Abuse," *Washington Times*, May 19, 2014.

11  Gen. 1:31.

12  Meeting with Artists, Address of His Holiness Benedict XVI, Sistine Chapel, November 21, 2009.

13  Pope John Paul II, *Man and Woman He Created Them: A Theology of the Body*, trans. Michael Waldstein (Boston: Pauline Books and Media, 2006), 13:1.

14  Cf. Mark 1:21–27.

15  Matt. 4:1–11.

16  Ignatius of Loyola, "Rules for the Discernment of Spirits," translated by Louis J. Puhl, S.J.

17  Prov. 31:30, NAB.

18  Sherry Turkle, *New York Times*, "The Flight from Conversation," April 21, 2012.

19  Matt. 6:33.

20  Heather Cicchese, *Boston Globe*, "College Class Tries to Revive the Lost Art of Dating," May 16, 2014.

21  Justin R. Garcia, et al. "Sexual Hookup Culture: A Review," *Review of General Psychology* 16:2 (2012):161–76.

22  E.L. Paul and K.E. Hayes, "The Casualties of 'Casual' Sex: A Qualitative Exploration of The Phenomenology of College Students' Hookups," *Journal of Social and Personal Relationships* 19 (2002): 639–61.

23  Janssen, et al., "Skeletal Muscle Mass and Distribution in 468 Men and Women Aged 18–88 Yr," *Journal of Applied Physiology* (July 1, 2000).

24  Leyk, et al., "Hand-Grip Strength of Young Men, Women and Highly Trained Female Athletes," *European Journal of Applied Physiology* 99:4 (2007): 415–21.

25  Linda Melone, "10 Reasons You Should Never Have Kids," MSN.com, September 1, 2015.

26  G.K. Chesterson, *What's Wrong with the World* (Ignatius Press: San Francisco, 1994).

27  Karol Wojtyła, *Love and Responsibility* (San Francisco: Ignatius Press, 1993), 128–29.

28  Ambrose Hollingworth Redmoon, "No Peaceful Warriors!," *Gnosis* 21 (Fall 1991).

29  Jason and Crystalina Evert, *A Guide to the Dating Project* (West Chester, Pa.: Ascension, 2018), 61.

30  Thucydides, "History of the Peloponnesian War."

31  John M. Szostak, *In the Footsteps of Pope John Paul II* (Englewood Cliffs, N.J.: Prentice-Hall, Inc., 1980), 18.

32  Dr. Timothy Patitsas, "Chastity and Empathy: Eros, Agape, and the Mystery of the Twofold Anointing," *Road to Emmaus* 1, no. 60 (Winter 2015).

33  Crockett, et al., "Restricting Temptations: Neural Mechanisms of Precommitment," *Neuron* 79:2 (July 24, 2013): 391–401.

34  Dietrich Bonhoeffer, quoted in Eric Metaxas, *Bonhoeffer: Pastor, Martyr, Prophet, Spy* (Nashville: Thomas Nelson, 2010), 486.

35  Confessions, Book VIII, chapter 7, 17.

36  Confessions, III, chapter 1.

37  Confessions, VI, chapter 11, 20.

38  Devin Schadt, *Joseph's Way: Sponsus* (Fathers of St. Joseph: United States, 2013), 27.

39  Matt. 26:41.

40  Saint Josemaría Escrivá, *Furrow* (New York: Scepter, 2002), 189.

41  *Love and Responsibility*, 143, 144.

42  Bonhoeffer, quoted in Metaxas, *Bonhoeffer*, 486.

43  Fulton J. Sheen, *Three to Get Married* (Princeton, N.J.: Scepter Publishers, Inc., 1951), 2.

44  Message of the Holy Father John Paul II to the Young People of Cuba, Camagüey, January 23, 1998.

45  Cf. Saint Francis de Sales, *Introduction to the Devout Life*, Chapter XX.

46  Eccles. 4:12–13.

47  Herbert J. Thurston, S.J., *Butler's Lives of the Saints*, Volume II (Westminster, Md.: Christian Classics, 1990), 541.

48  John 14:1–3.

49  Cardinal Joseph Ratzinger, *God and the World* (San Francisco: Ignatius Press, 2002), 258.

50  Devin Schadt, "The Meaning of Man: The Theological Location and Essence of the Masculine Nature in the Cosmos."

51  Bill Adler, ed., *The Wit & Wisdom of Bishop Fulton J. Sheen* (New York: Image Books, 1969).

52  C.S. Lewis, *The Weight of Glory* (New York: Harper One, 2001), 31.

53  Cf. Matt. 19:9.

54  Fulton Sheen, *Calvary and the Mass* (New York: IVE Press, 2008), 75.

55  *Letters of J.R.R. Tolkien*, 51–52.

56  Fr. John A. Hardon, S.J., *Saint Peter Claver: Jesuit Saint* (Inter Mirifica, 1998).

57  2 Macc. 7:3–6.

58  Heb. 12:6, NAB.

59  Saint Augustine, *On the Teacher*, 11, 37.

60  Saint Fidelis of Sigmaringen, as quoted in Jill Haak Adels, *The Wisdom of the Saints* (New York: Oxford University Press, 1987), 48.

61  Job 36:15.

62  1 Cor. 10:13.

63  Phil. 1:6.

64  Archives of Padre Pio.

65  Alice von Hildebrand, "Love, Marriage and Faithfulness in Søren Kierkegaard," Philosophy Readings Manual, Dr. Michael Healy, ed. (Steubenville, Oh.: Franciscan University Press, 1974).

66  Saint Francis DeSales, *Letters to Persons in the World*, I, 8.

67  Karol Wojtyła, *The Way to Christ* (New York: Harper & Row, 1984), 80.

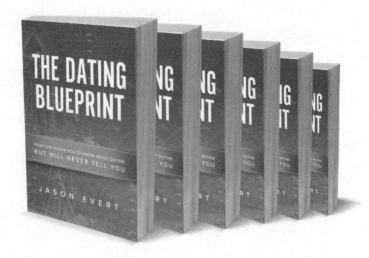

## Share *THE DATING BLUEPRINT* with others for as little as
# $3 per copy!

Think of those in your community who could benefit from reading it:

- Start a book study in your college dorm
- Give it away in your youth or young adult group
- Share copies with your Confirmation or religious ed classmates
- Study it in your high school religion class
- Distribute copies on retreats
- Offer it as a gift for graduations and birthdays
- Donate copies to your campus ministry program

### For more information, visit
## chastity.com